WHERE'S YOUR DADDY

Healing the Wounds of Fatherlessness Through Faith and Community

Bishop Cornelius Bowser

For permissions contact:
cornelius.bowser@shaphat.org
Cornelius Bowser
900 N. Cuyamaca Street Ste. 103
El Cajon, CA 92020
www.corneliusbowser-gangs.com

Printed Worldwide
First Printing 2025
First Edition 2025
ISBN: 979-8-9925806-0-0

TABLE OF CONTENTS

Introduction 1

Chapter 1
The Role of the Father... 3

Chapter 2
The Absence and Its Roots 15

Chapter 3
Reconstructing Masculinity 24

Chapter 4
Relationships and Interpersonal Dynamics 42

Chapter 5
Reasserting Masculinity in Leadership 59

Chapter 6
Pathways to Healing and Growth.. 78

Chapter 7
Healing For Our Black Fathers 90

Chapter 8
Community Violence And The Black Family........................103

Chapter 9
Liberating the Soul of Black Manhood................................. 112

Chapter 10
Fathers and Sons Rising.. 121

Epilogue
Embracing the Journey.. 135

INTRODUCTION

In the tapestry of life, the presence of a father often serves as a critical thread, weaving a sense of identity, stability, and emotional support into the fabric of a young man's upbringing. Yet, for many in the Black community, this vital thread remains conspicuously absent. "Where's Your Daddy" embarks on a profound exploration of the multifaceted impact of fatherlessness, inviting readers to engage with the complexities faced by individuals navigating a world without paternal figures. As we delve into the implications for boys and young men, we confront the harsh realities of emotional development, identity formation, and the shaping of relationships in the absence of a father.

In our ever-evolving society, the notion of family and the roles within it has undergone significant transformation. The absence of paternal figures is not just a personal tragedy; it permeates the very fabric of communities, influencing everything from childhood experiences to adult relationships. Fathers play an indispensable role in shaping identity, guiding emotional development, and providing stability. Without these guiding hands, many boys and young men find themselves grappling with questions about masculinity and self-worth in a world that often leaves them to navigate uncharted waters alone.

The purpose of this book is to shine a light on the often-overlooked challenges that arise when young men grow up without male role models. Readers will gain insights into how the absence of a father impacts the lives of young black men and boys, shaping their behavior, self-expression, and understanding of masculinity. In a society that frequently imposes rigid definitions of manhood, many boys feel pressured to adjust their identities in ways that may not reflect their true selves. This perspective draws from my experiences working with and growing up alongside these young individuals.

Statistics reveal a troubling reality: according to the U.S. Census Bureau, nearly 50% of Black children grow up without a father in the home. Numerous studies have shown that such a father's absence is associated with higher rates of poverty, emotional distress, behavioral issues, and lower educational attainment. These statistics serve as a foundation for understanding the critical need for male presence and guidance in the lives of young boys — not just to fulfill a role, but to encourage healthy emotional development and self-acceptance.

By engaging with these themes throughout "Where's Your Daddy," we will seek to challenge societal notions of masculinity and femininity, redefining what it means to be a man in contemporary society. We aim to inspire a movement towards healing — highlighting the importance of community involvement and the cultivation of supportive relationships that can empower young men to thrive despite the absence of their fathers.

In our exploration, we will seek to understand the challenges faced by those affected by fatherlessness, as well as potential pathways to resilience and growth. Welcome to a conversation that is both timely and necessary— a journey to discover not just where our fathers are, but where we can go from here.

CHAPTER 1
THE ROLE OF THE FATHER

Fathers play a crucial role in shaping families and society, serving not only as authority figures but also as spiritual guides. Traditionally, the father has been viewed as the head of the household, a figure of strength and guidance established under divine authority. However, this authority must never be misconstrued as a license for verbal, psychological, or physical abuse. A true father leads with love, respect, and a sense of responsibility, setting the foundation for a nurturing environment.

The Authority of a Father

In many cultures, the father's role as the head of the house comes with expectations and responsibilities that are both significant and multifaceted. A father is tasked with not just authority but also a moral obligation to lead his family in alignment with ethical standards and spiritual principles. This leadership should be rooted in love and care, creating a household where respect is mutual, and where children can flourish in an environment free from abuse or harm.

The Psychological and Emotional Functions of Fathers in the Black Experience

The psychological and emotional contributions of fathers to family life are profoundly impactful, particularly within the context of the Black experience. Fathers offer stability and confidence and serve as essential models for emotional expression, shaping not just the present but also the future of their children. For Black families, where historical and societal challenges often add layers of complexity to family dynamics, the role of the father becomes even more crucial. Within these families, fathers play a pivotal role in reinforcing their children's sense of worth and value amid external pressures, confirming their right to thrive in a world that may often question it.

In a child's development, the presence of a father provides a reassuring foundation of love and support. This emotional stability fosters trust and safety, enabling children to explore their identities and the world around them with assurance. The act of witnessing healthy affection and balanced authority from fathers instills important life lessons; children learn to emulate traits of love, respect, and emotional honesty. These traits become critical building blocks for their own identities, allowing them to navigate relationships and societal expectations with resilience and confidence.

Fathers serve as primary role models, showcasing how to handle complex emotions and emphasizing the importance of moral integrity, honesty, and accountability. In the context of the Black family, where systemic issues may have historically challenged their standing, the father's role is to counteract narratives of inadequacy and empower their children to express their feelings openly and constructively. This modeling isn't simply about providing tools for emotional expression but also about imparting a sense of pride in their heritage and identity.

The impact of a father's active involvement in their children's lives cannot be overstated. When fathers express affection, encourage open dialogue, and validate their children's feelings, they cultivate emotionally rich lives, setting the stage for self-esteem and psychological well-being. This active engagement teaches children that their emotions are valid, establishing a precedent for healthy emotional communication and interaction with others. This is crucial in a society where norms may discourage vulnerability, especially for Black boys who often face societal pressures to conform to rigid notions of masculinity.

Furthermore, the bond forged through emotional availability serves as a resilient foundation upon which children can build self-worth, creativity, and social competence. A father who is present and engaged provides not only physical protection but also spiritual and emotional guardianship, allowing children to confront the world with a strong sense of identity and purpose. In a culture that has long sought to erode Black families through stereotypes and marginalization, the emotional strength that fathers impart becomes a vital resistance against those narratives.

Ultimately, the psychological and emotional functions of fathers in the Black experience are deeply intertwined with broader narratives of identity, resilience, and empowerment. By fostering an environment of love, security, and emotional literacy, fathers not only challenge societal expectations but also cultivate a legacy of strength and self-affirmation. In doing so, they prepare their children to face the world with confidence and grace, carrying forward the rich heritage of their ancestors while forging their own paths. This legacy is not just about survival; it's about thriving, demonstrating that the emotional and psychological contributions of fathers are indispensable to the holistic development of their children and the community at large.

Societal Expectations of Masculinity and the Role of Black Fathers

Societal expectations of masculinity significantly complicate the role of Black fathers in modern families. Traditional notions of masculinity often prioritize strength, stoicism, and emotional restraint—views that can confine Black men to a narrow framework for expressing themselves. These outdated ideals create barriers to emotional vulnerability, leading some fathers to suppress their feelings and avoid meaningful emotional exchanges with their children. This perpetuation of the "tough man" stereotype not only reinforces harmful narratives but also risks leaving children without essential emotional guidance.

However, there is a growing movement among Black fathers toward redefining masculinity in a way that honors their profound emotional capacities. Today's societal landscape increasingly encourages emotional expression, especially in the context of fatherhood. An emotionally intelligent Black father cultivates an environment of safety and openness, where children feel free to articulate their feelings and concerns. By challenging traditional barriers and reshaping the definition of masculinity, Black fathers can nurture emotionally healthy and resilient children, equipping them to navigate life's challenges with compassion and strength.

At the heart of this transformation is the concept of holiness and moral purity. For many Black fathers, living a life grounded in integrity, devotion, and adherence to spiritual principles is essential for imparting values that transcend societal expectations. Holiness becomes a universal aspiration, guiding family life and influencing how fathers lead and interact with their children.

The principle of holiness emphasizes a commitment to moral values such as integrity, honesty, and service to others. This way of living fosters a profound sense of responsibility, respect, and love within the family unit. Children raised in this environment are more likely to develop a strong ethical foundation, helping them understand the importance of moral purity in their daily interactions. Black fathers who embody these principles demonstrate that true strength lies not in emotional suppression but in the courage to express love, compassion, and understanding—a vital lesson for children growing up amid a world that can be critical and unyielding.

Moreover, the concept of masculinity often burdens Black men with rigid expectations that can be damaging. Society imposes a narrow definition of what it means to be a man, leading young Black boys to conform to ideals that may clash with their true selves. This pressure can result in emotional suppression and a disconnect from their identities, perpetuating cycles of frustration and misunderstanding.

Black fathers have a unique opportunity to redefine these expectations and guide their sons toward a more holistic understanding of masculinity— one that embraces strength, vulnerability, and compassion. By modeling emotional openness and demonstrating that it is acceptable to express feelings, these fathers can counter harmful narratives that dictate masculinity and empower their children to develop a lasting sense of self-worth.

By embracing a more nuanced understanding of masculinity, Black fathers can create an environment that nurtures emotional openness and overall development. They serve as role models who exemplify that vulnerability is not a weakness but a pathway toward deeper connections and resilience. This redefined masculinity benefits not only Black fathers and their children but also contributes to a healthier society—one where emotional well-being, ethical integrity, and authentic self-expression are valued over outdated stereotypes. Through their commitment to fostering these values, Black fathers can help build a legacy of strength and compassion in their families and communities, ensuring that their children are prepared to navigate a complex world with confidence and grace.

Responsibilities of a Father:
Leadership in the Context of the Black Experience

At the core of a father's role lies the profound responsibility of leadership within the family. This responsibility extends beyond merely providing for their physical needs; it encompasses nurturing their emotional and spiritual well-being as well. In 1 Timothy 5:8 (NIV), we find a compelling directive: "Anyone who does not provide for their relatives, especially for their own household, has denied the faith and is worse than an unbeliever." This scripture underscores the sacred obligation of a father to ensure the economic stability of the family while also fostering their spiritual growth.

For Black fathers, this leadership role is often confronted with unique challenges rooted in systemic forces and institutional barriers that seek to undermine their authority. Historically, societal structures have sought to emasculate Black men by stripping them of their power, dignity, and the ability to fulfill their roles as head of the household. From the legacy of slavery, which violently disrupted family structures, to contemporary issues like mass incarceration, racial discrimination, and economic inequality, the Black experience is frequently marked by forces that challenge the traditional family dynamic and the father's role within it.

These systemic challenges create an environment where Black fathers must navigate not only the responsibilities of parenthood but also the societal perceptions that often devalue their authority. Institutions such as the criminal justice system and economic structures have been designed in ways that disproportionately affect Black communities, creating barriers to stable employment and family cohesion. The impact of these systems can lead to feelings of helplessness and frustration among Black fathers, who may find themselves working against forces that diminish their ability to lead effectively and provide for their families.

Despite these obstacles, many Black fathers rise to the occasion, embodying resilience and determination. They are tasked with the critical role of instilling values of strength, integrity, and emotional intelligence in their children, often drawing from their own experiences of facing and overcoming adversity. By embracing their roles with conviction, Black fathers not only challenge the narratives that seek to emasculate them but also redefine what it means to be a leader within their families and communities.

In nurturing their children's emotional and spiritual growth, Black fathers cultivate an environment of love, respect, and support. They model for their children the importance of advocating for oneself and maintaining dignity, even in the face of societal obstacles. Through open dialogue about race, identity, and resilience, they equip their children with the tools to navigate a world that may not always recognize their worth.

Ultimately, the leadership role of Black fathers is not just about fulfilling traditional expectations, but about reclaiming authority and dignity in a society that often undermines them. By focusing on their responsibilities as providers and nurturers, Black fathers can foster family environments that challenge systemic narratives and empower the next generation. This commitment to leadership—rooted in love, resilience, and faith—ensures that their families can thrive even amidst adversity, breaking the cycles of emasculation and fostering a legacy of strength and unity that transcends generations.

Love for His Wife and The Foundation of Family Stability

A father's responsibilities extend profoundly to how he treats his wife, as the strength of their relationship forms the bedrock of a family's stability. His love must embody a selfless commitment, echoing the call in Ephesians 5:25 (NIV): "Husbands, love your wives, just as Christ loved the church and gave himself up for her." This self-sacrificial love involves putting aside personal interests for the sake of his wife's happiness and well-being, embodying the essence of true partnership.

In the context of Black culture, which is rich and diverse but often influenced by the portrayals in hip-hop, reality shows, and celebrity lifestyles, the understanding of love can sometimes be distorted. While these cultural elements can provide entertainment and education, they do not always present the healthiest models of loving relationships. Many of the narratives found within these mediums—whether it's the glamorization of infidelity, superficial relationships, or financial exploitation—can perpetuate unhealthy expectations about love and marriage.

It's crucial for Black men to seek a genuine relationship with Yahweh to understand what true love is. In doing so, they can cultivate a deeper and more meaningful connection with their wives. By turning to spiritual teachings and the example set by Christ, Black fathers can learn that love is not about dominance or fulfillment of one's ego but about mutual respect, nurturing, and support.

In Ephesians 5:29 (NIV), we are reminded, "After all, no one ever hated their own body, but they feed and care for their body, just as Christ does the church." This metaphor emphasizes the importance of cherishing and nourishing one's partner. A truly loving relationship recognizes that the health of the marital bond directly impacts the family's overall stability. When a father treats his wife with kindness and respect, he sets an example for his children about the importance of healthy relationships.

For Black men, embracing this understanding of love means actively rejecting the fragmentary models portrayed in popular culture. It involves consciously choosing to build a strong, respectful foundation with their wives, rooted in shared faith and commitment. True love requires vulnerability and emotional investment, leading to an environment where both partners feel valued and supported.

By prioritizing their relationship with Yahweh and allowing that relationship to inform how they love their wives, Black fathers can break free from the constraints imposed by cultural stereotypes. They can show their families what real love looks like—characterized by sacrifice, vulnerability, and unwavering support. This not only strengthens their marriages but also fosters a nurturing environment for their children, teaching them the principles of respect, kindness, and partnership.

The love a father shows to his wife is pivotal in shaping a stable family unit. By seeking a relationship with Yahweh and understanding the essence of true love, Black fathers can navigate the complexities of their cultural landscape and model healthy relationships. This journey toward selflessness and genuine affection will not only enrich their marriages but also leave an indelible mark on the future generation, instilling in them a robust understanding of love that reflects Christ's example.

A Father's Role in the Modern Context

A father serves as a vital protector of his family, safeguarding them from both physical and emotional harm. This protective role encompasses more than mere physical security; it requires providing emotional and psychological support that uplifts children, meets their needs, and encourages their endeavors. By being present and engaged, a father fosters resilience within the family unit, allowing all members to thrive.

However, for many Black men, the struggle to fulfill this protective role is compounded by systemic challenges and societal pressures. Many Black fathers find themselves navigating a world where they are often treated differently—whether they are on probation or parole or simply experiencing the day-to-day reality of being stopped by law enforcement. These interactions can be fraught with tension, leaving many men feeling vulnerable and anxious about their ability to protect their families.

Additionally, the challenges can extend beyond external forces. Within their own communities, Black men may encounter a spectrum of threats, both from individuals who may not have the same commitment to peace and from a culture that can sometimes glorify violence as a means of protection. When faced with constant societal pressures and intimidation, the instinct to shield loved ones can lead some fathers to resort to choices rooted in violence or intimidation, further complicating their ability to provide a loving and safe home.

The absence of Black men in church and in active service to God can exacerbate this situation. When spiritual guidance and community support are lacking, fathers may struggle to find constructive ways to protect their families beyond aggressive or defensive tactics. Engaging with faith can provide the moral compass needed to navigate these challenges, reminding fathers of their roles as loving providers and protectors, as modeled by God.

In Isaiah 38:19 (NKJV), we are reminded of the father's duty to pass down truth and wisdom: "The living, the living man, he shall praise You; as I do this day; the father shall make known Your truth to the children." This call for spiritual guidance emphasizes that a father is meant to act not just as a protector of the body, but also as a steward of faith and values. Through his example and teachings, he can impart wisdom that equips his children to make informed choices about life, faith, and relationships.

To genuinely fulfill the role of protector, Black fathers must transcend the knee-jerk reactions shaped by their circumstances. By actively seeking a relationship with God, they can find the strength and guidance to protect their families in a manner that aligns with true love and spiritual principles. This journey towards understanding and embodying God's vision of protection allows fathers to lead their families away from cycles of violence and despair, fostering an environment where love, respect, and resilience can flourish.

The protective role of a father is multifaceted, involving physical, emotional, and spiritual dimensions. For Black fathers facing unique societal challenges, it is essential to seek a higher purpose in their protective instincts. By anchoring themselves in faith and spiritual practice, they can redefine how they show love and provide security, ultimately fostering a safe and nurturing environment for their families to thrive.

Spiritual Role in Serving Yahweh

The spiritual dimension of fatherhood is of utmost importance, particularly in the context of serving Yahweh through faith in Jesus Christ. A father's role as a spiritual leader is foundational to nurturing a child's understanding of faith and developing a relationship with God. In a world where so many uncertainties abound, fathers are called to guide their families toward truth, instilling the values of faith and hope.

According to Deuteronomy 6:6-7, fathers are instructed to impress God's commands upon their children, talking about them at home and when they walk along the road when they lie down, and when they get up. This continual engagement in spiritual discussions creates an environment where faith can flourish. It empowers children to understand the importance of a relationship with God, one that can provide comfort during challenging times and offer guidance throughout their lives.

Furthermore, the presence of a father living out his faith in practical ways serves as an embodiment of Christ's teachings. When fathers model prayer, worship, and community engagement, they show their children how to live out their beliefs authentically. This alignment of faith in everyday life creates a legacy of faith that has the potential to echo through generations.

The father serves not only as a nourisher of faith but also as the family's priest. Ephesians 6:4 (NIV) instructs, "Fathers, do not exasperate your children; instead, bring them up in the training and instruction of the Lord." This implies that the father's responsibility includes guiding his children through both discipline and love, helping them understand the significance of their faith, and encouraging them to cultivate their own relationship with God.

The Essential Role of the Black Father

A father's role as a nourisher of his family transcends mere provision; it encompasses fostering spiritual, mental, and emotional growth in his children. Ephesians 6:4 (NIV) instructs us: "Fathers, do not exasperate your children; instead, bring them up in the training and instruction of the Lord." This passage highlights a nurturing approach that prioritizes development over discipline, encouraging fathers to cultivate a love for learning, exploration, and personal growth in their children.

In the context of the Black family, it's important to recognize that many fathers are present but not deeply engaged in their children's lives. While they may be physically around, their emotional and intellectual involvement often falls short. This lack of engagement can stem from a variety of factors, including socio-economic pressures, overwhelming responsibilities, or a systemic absence of supportive community structures. Fathers may struggle with how to connect meaningfully with their children amid these challenges, which can lead to feelings of frustration or inadequacy.

To nurture their children effectively, Black fathers must strive to break away from just being present and embrace active participation in their children's lives. This means not only attending events or being physically available but also engaging in conversations that inspire curiosity, encouraging them in their academic pursuits, and being a source of emotional support. By investing time in their children's personal development, they create an atmosphere rich with opportunities for exploration and growth.

The vital role of nourishment also extends into spiritual guidance, as fathers are encouraged to lead by example. By demonstrating faith and imparting spiritual wisdom, they can help their children develop a strong moral foundation and a sense of purpose. Engagement in family worship, prayer, and community involvement can foster a nurturing environment where children feel secure and valued.

In summary, the roles and responsibilities of fathers are profound and far-reaching, encompassing authority, love, protection, nourishment, and spiritual guidance. They have the power to shape their children's identities and break cycles of disconnection that can arise from both physical absence and emotional disengagement.

Fathers can redefine masculinity and cultivate balanced, caring, emotionally intelligent future generations by being deeply involved in their lives. As we continue to examine the impact of fatherlessness, it is essential to highlight the significance of both presence and active participation. Understanding the traditional and spiritual roles of fathers helps us grasp the void created when these figures are not fully engaged, urging us to seek alternative pathways toward resilience and growth for those affected.

Ultimately, the call to action for Black fathers is clear: embrace the fullness of their roles as nourishing and instructive figures in their children's lives. This commitment will not only enrich their families but also contribute to a more robust, supportive community that uplifts everyone.

CHAPTER 2
THE ABSENCE AND ITS ROOTS

The absence of fathers in the Black community is a multifaceted issue rooted in a complex interplay of historical, socio-economic, and cultural factors. Understanding these underlying elements is essential to address the pervasive consequences of father absence and to foster meaningful solutions. In this chapter, we will delve into the historical injustices, economic challenges, and cultural shifts that have contributed to the current state of father absence in the Black community.

Historical Context

The legacy of slavery in the United States has cast a long shadow over Black families, profoundly affecting family structures and roles. During slavery, Black fathers were often stripped of their paternal rights; families were routinely torn apart, and fathers were sold away from their children. This brutal historical context created generational trauma that persists today, fostering a culture of instability and mistrust in family dynamics.

Following emancipation, the effects of systemic racism and segregation continued to disrupt the Black family structure. Policies like Jim Crow laws enforced a social order that marginalized Black individuals, limiting their opportunities for economic advancement and stable family life. Over time, these systemic barriers contributed to cycles of poverty and dislocation, perpetuating a narrative wherein the father's role was increasingly compromised and diminished.

Socio-Economic Factors

In contemporary society, socio-economic challenges play a significant role in the absence of fathers within the Black community. Structural inequalities such as inadequate access to quality education, employment opportunities, and affordable housing continue to disproportionately affect Black families. The lack of stable jobs and fair wages can lead to financial strain, making it increasingly difficult for fathers to fulfill their roles as providers.

Additionally, the impact of mass incarceration cannot be overstated. Black men are disproportionately represented in the criminal justice system, a reality stemming from systemic biases and inequities. The phenomenon of mass incarceration has not only removed large numbers of fathers from their homes but has also created a cycle of disenfranchisement that makes reintegration into society challenging. Upon release, many men face barriers to employment, housing, and social services, further complicating their ability to reconnect with their families.

Cultural Factors

Culturally, narratives surrounding masculinity and fatherhood in the Black community have evolved significantly in response to a combination of historical and socio-economic challenges. The trauma associated with a father's absence has, in many instances, led to a normalization of this experience, creating a troubling cycle that is hard to break. Young boys who grow up without paternal figures often internalize the message that fatherhood is optional or laden with emotional and societal risks. They may come to see involvement as an unattainable or undesirable aspiration, perpetuating a cycle of absence that robs future generations of positive father figures.

The influence of subcultures, particularly those shaped by gangs and the drug trade, further complicates this narrative. In some communities, "gang life" can become an enticing alternative to traditional family structures.

Many young men are drawn into gangs, seeking a sense of belonging and identity that they may not find in their home environments. This often results in a diversion from the path of responsible fatherhood and further reinforces the perception that being a father is secondary to survival and loyalty to a street culture. The seductive nature of this lifestyle can lead to risky behaviors that jeopardize family bonds, creating environments where father absence becomes a norm.

Additionally, the War on Drugs has disproportionately impacted Black communities, leading to mass incarceration and the disruption of family structures. Many fathers are imprisoned due to drug-related offenses, separating them from their children and stripping families of their primary breadwinners and caregivers. This systemic issue has not only contributed to father absence but has also instilled a sense of hopelessness, making it difficult for children to envision a different future or hold onto aspirations of family involvement.

Media representations significantly shape societal perceptions of Black fathers, often portraying them as absent, ineffective, or even dangerous. These stereotypes overshadow the countless men who strive to be active, engaged parents and involved community members. Such negative portrayals reinforce harmful narratives that marginalize Black men, complicating their efforts to challenge these societal views and assert their roles as committed fathers within their families and communities.

As we examine these cultural factors, it becomes clear that addressing the absence of fathers in the Black community requires a nuanced understanding of the challenges posed by both systemic barriers and cultural narratives. By fostering positive representations of Black fatherhood in media and culture, and by addressing the socio-economic factors that contribute to these issues, we can work toward dismantling stereotypes and creating a more empowering narrative for future generations.

Moving Forward

To address the absence of fathers in the Black community, we must first acknowledge and analyze these historical, socio-economic, and cultural factors. Solutions must be multifaceted and holistic, encompassing education, economic empowerment, mental health support, and community engagement. By creating a supportive environment that promotes positive fatherhood and challenges prevailing stereotypes, we can work toward healing generational wounds and fostering a future where Black fathers are not only present but empowered to thrive.

By diving deep into these roots, we can better understand the complexity of father absence and pave the way for effective interventions and supportive structures that uplift Black families. The journey toward a more vibrant, connected, and nurturing community begins with recognizing the obstacles and striving collectively to dismantle them. As we progress through this exploration, it is crucial to remember that the story of Black fatherhood is not solely one of absence but also one filled with resilience, potential, and hope for future generations.

Incarceration, Poverty, and Racism

The challenges facing the Black community today cannot be understood in isolation; they are deeply intertwined with systemic issues such as incarceration, poverty, and racism. These interconnected factors perpetuate a cycle of disadvantage that makes it extraordinarily difficult for families to thrive.

Incarceration and Over-Policing

A significant driver of father absence in the Black community is the disproportionately high rate of incarceration among Black men, largely a result of systemic racism and aggressive law enforcement practices. Over-policing and racial profiling contribute to this dilemma, where Black individuals are more frequently subjected to stop-and-frisk rules and pretext stops, often without just cause. The San Diego State University (SDSU) Traffic Stop report vividly illustrates this reality: young Black drivers were found to be 43.8% more likely to be stopped during daylight hours than their white counterparts, and they were subjected to field interviews over 82% more than matched white drivers from 2014 to 2015.

Such practices erode trust between law enforcement and the community, cultivating an environment of fear and resentment. The

American Journal of Public Health highlights that police encounters based on procedural justice—where individuals are treated fairly and with respect—can have a positive impact on community relations. However, the current state of over-policing often fosters hostility rather than harmony, pushing communities further apart.

Poverty and A Structural Barrier

Poverty compounds the effects of incarceration and over-policing, creating an environment where opportunities for growth and stability are scarce. Many Black families live in neighborhoods that are economically disadvantaged, lacking access to quality education, healthcare, and employment. This financial instability not only strains family units but also perpetuates a cycle of hopelessness. Children growing up in these environments are often deprived of essential resources, further diminishing the likelihood that they will break free from these cycles. The sentiment echoed in the Apostle James's exhortation in James 3:17-18 (MSG), "You can develop a healthy, robust community that lives right with God and enjoys its results only if you do the hard work of getting along with each other, treating each other with dignity and honor," underscores the necessity for mutual respect and cooperation in overcoming these systemic challenges.

Racism Is An Uphill Battle

At the core of these issues is an insidious structure of systemic racism that permeates every aspect of life for Black Americans. Vulnerability to discrimination affects employment opportunities, wages, education, and interactions with law enforcement. This systemic racism is not merely an individual failing but a societal one that imposes barriers to success and stability for entire communities. Romans 12:18 (NIV) reminds us, "If it is possible, as far as it depends on you, live at peace with everyone." Achieving peace requires effort from all parties involved, balancing the responsibility to address grievances with a commitment to building mutual understanding.

For peace to take root, a genuine dialogue must emerge between communities and law enforcement. This conversation should focus on identifying the conditions necessary for restoring trust and advancing equity. However, the rejection of reform initiatives—such as those I presented to the City of San Diego's Citizens Advisory Board on Police/Community Relations, which called for the abolition of the Gang Suppression Team (while maintaining the San Diego Police Gang Investigative Unit) and the implementation of procedural justice practices—reveals a reluctance within our governing systems to acknowledge and address these pervasive issues.

James 2:9 (NLT) further illuminates the sin of favoritism: "But if you favor some people over others, you are committing a sin. You are guilty of breaking the law." The current policing practices resonate with this sentiment, revealing a clear bias against particular groups that requires urgent and unwavering attention.

Moving Toward Solutions

Ultimately, addressing these systemic issues requires a multifaceted approach that involves reforming law enforcement practices, ensuring equitable access to education and economic opportunities, and dismantling the structures that perpetuate racism. Collectively, we must advocate for policies that discourage racial profiling and support criminal justice reforms to reduce incarceration rates. As a community of believers and change-makers, we can aspire to cultivate a society where mutual respect and dignity serve as the foundation for our interactions, enabling us to build the robust and thriving community that James speaks of.

It is within this context of interdependence and collaboration that we can harness our efforts toward lasting change. The work demands perseverance and commitment, and by standing together, we can define the conditions necessary for peace and equality, allowing every individual to contribute fully to the betterment of our shared society.

The Impact of Single-Parent Households

The structure of family units plays a crucial role in shaping the social, economic, and emotional landscapes for children. Currently, approximately 60% to 61% of Black American children are raised in single-parent households, a statistic that starkly contrasts with the rates in other ethnic groups. For instance, only 23% of non-Latino white children, 14% to 15% of Asian children, and 32% to 33% of Latino children live in single-parent families. Native

American communities also experience a noteworthy percentage, though exact figures may vary. Understanding the implications of these figures is essential for addressing the broader societal issues faced by communities operating within this family structure.

Contributing Factors to High Single-Parent Households Among Black Americans

According to Save America Ministries in their 2017 Edition: A Portrait of the Black Family, the statistics reveal a troubling reality: approximately 72% of all Black children are born out of wedlock. Marriage among Black Americans has increasingly been perceived as an "alternative lifestyle," with many considering it "nonessential," as noted by Andrew Lyke, Coordinator of Marriage Ministry for the Archdiocese of Chicago. This shift in perception indicates deeper societal issues at play.

Dr. Beverly Guy-Sheftall, a leading scholar on gender relations, highlights that while Black women often assume marriage will be monogamous, many Black men do not attach the same significance to monogamous relationships. This disparity contributes to a profound level of distrust between young Black men and women, leading to what Dr. Guy-Sheftall describes as "an acute crisis" in Black sexual politics, which has created a visible schism in male and female relations within the community.

The consequences of these dynamics are stark. Nearly two million Black males are either currently incarcerated or have experienced incarceration. Furthermore, over 80% of long-term child poverty occurs in broken or never-married homes, with a staggering 85 out of 100 Black children from such households living in poverty. Alarmingly, 70% of Black males in the criminal justice system come from single-parent homes, pointing to a direct correlation between family structure and involvement with the judicial system. Additionally, 85% of Black children do not reside in a household with their fathers, a statistic that highlights the fragmentation of families across the community. Of those living in poverty, 85% reside in single-parent households.

Several intertwined factors contribute to the elevated prevalence of single-parent households in the Black American community. One significant reason is the relatively low marriage rate, which currently stands at about 29.9%. This low rate is influenced by a range of economic challenges, social barriers, and historical factors that have consistently shaped family dynamics.

In addition to the low marriage rate, the Black American community suffers from a higher separation and divorce rate compared to other demographic groups. This trend is rooted in historical disparities and has been exacerbated by a variety of structural and systemic issues, including the enduring legacy of slavery and ongoing racial discrimination. These factors have contributed to economic instability and social fragmentation, making it increasingly difficult for many families to maintain intact structures.

The interplay of these elements creates a challenging environment for children, often perpetuating cycles of poverty, distrust, and instability. It is essential to address these challenges through targeted interventions and supportive policies that promote family stability, economic empowerment, and meaningful relationships within the Black American community. Only by confronting these issues head-on can meaningful progress be made toward improving outcomes for children and families alike.

Economic Challenges Faced by Single-Parent Households

The economic difficulties faced by single-parent households, especially those led by single mothers, cannot be overlooked. Many single-parent families experience heightened financial strain due to a reliance on a single income. This economic vulnerability can severely limit access to essential resources, such as quality education, healthcare, and stable housing—factors critical to child development and well-being.

Research indicates that children from single-parent households are at a higher risk of encountering adverse outcomes, including lower academic performance, increased behavioral issues, and diminished access to extracurricular opportunities. The absence of a second parent often translates into less financial and emotional support, which can impede a child's ability to thrive in various aspects of life.

Furthermore, single mothers often face the dual challenge of balancing work and child-rearing responsibilities without the assistance of a partner. This multifaceted strain can lead to elevated stress levels and resultant negative effects on parenting. The challenges are compounded by systemic issues, including discriminatory employment practices and economic disparities that disproportionately affect Black American families, placing them at an even greater disadvantage.

Broader Societal Implications

The impact of high rates of single-parent households extends beyond the individual family unit, influencing broader societal dynamics. Children from single-parent families often face challenges that diminish their opportunities for upward mobility, perpetuating cycles of poverty. This generational disadvantage is not just a personal or familial issue; it is a societal problem that requires collective attention and action.

Community resources, public policy, and social programs that support family stability, economic empowerment, and educational opportunities are crucial to addressing these disparities. By working to alleviate the economic and social challenges that lead to single-parent households, society can foster an environment where all families, regardless of structure, have equal opportunities to thrive.

The high prevalence of single-parent households among Black Americans, largely the result of low marriage rates, economic challenges, and historical factors, has significant implications for children and the community at large. Understanding these dynamics is essential for crafting effective policies and support systems aimed at promoting family stability and improving outcomes for children. Addressing these issues requires a collaborative approach that encompasses community involvement, equitable policy-making, and targeted interventions designed to empower single-parent families and enhance the opportunities available to their children.

CHAPTER 3
RECONSTRUCTING MASCULINITY

The concept of masculinity has long been a complex and evolving subject, shaped by social norms, cultural expectations, and individual experiences. As society grapples with redefining gender roles, it has become increasingly evident that the absence of fathers, particularly Black fathers, within families significantly influences boys' self-perception and identity. The father-son dynamic is pivotal in shaping a boy's understanding of what it means to be a man. When this relationship is disrupted—whether through physical absence, emotional unavailability, or societal factors—boys may struggle to develop a coherent sense of self, often resorting to external influences, including the behaviors of their mothers, to fill the void left by their fathers.

In examining the implications of father absence, it is essential to highlight the unique challenges faced by many Black boys today. Historically, systemic inequalities have impacted Black fathers disproportionately, leading to higher rates of incarceration, unemployment, and family separation. This absence can create a significant emotional and psychological burden for boys, often resulting in them mimicking the coping mechanisms and behaviors of their mothers instead of developing a balanced male identity shaped by the presence of a father. While mothers play an incredibly influential role in nurturing and upbringing, the lack of a paternal figure can hinder boys from accessing critical masculine models for self-expression and identity formation.

In contemporary discussions surrounding masculinity, the challenge remains of how boys navigate their identities in the absence of paternal figures. The emotional ramifications are often profound and can lead to various developmental challenges—ranging from emotional struggles and behavioral issues to difficulties in forming healthy relationships as they mature. Without a father or father figure to model masculine behavior, boys are frequently left to construct their identities from a hodgepodge of societal messages, peer influences, and media representations. Unfortunately, many of these sources reinforce outdated stereotypes rather than promoting healthy, multifaceted expressions of manhood.

This chapter seeks to investigate the deep-seated effects of father absence on boys' self-perception and identity, particularly within the context of Black fatherhood. By examining the critical role that fathers play in a boy's life, we can gain insights into their development of self-worth, emotional intelligence, and conceptions of masculinity. Furthermore, we will explore how these impacts can lead to various coping mechanisms and behavioral adaptations that can be constructive or detrimental.

Additionally, inherent within Black boys' experiences is a struggle to reconcile maternal influences with the absence of paternal guidance. Many Black boys raised in single-mother households may adopt coping strategies that mimic their mothers' ways of navigating the world, which can sometimes clash with societal ideals of masculinity. This bifurcation can lead to confusion about what it means to be a man, limiting boys' emotional expression to what they observe rather than reflecting a balanced understanding of masculine and feminine qualities.

As we delve deep into this subject, it is vital to approach it holistically by considering factors such as socioeconomic conditions, cultural narratives, and psychological theories. This comprehensive understanding will enable us to identify potential pathways for reconstructing masculine identities for boys who grow up without active paternal involvement. Through this reconstruction, we can foster healthier, more positive expressions of manhood for future generations, helping boys navigate their identities in a manner that honors both their experiences and their aspirations.

The Impact of Father Absence on Black Boys' Self-Perception and Identity
The Role of Fathers in Identity Development

For Black boys, the role of fathers as primary role models is particularly significant. Fathers provide crucial insights into masculine identity and behavioral expectations, helping their sons navigate the complexities of their cultural and social environments. The interactions between fathers and sons are foundational to the construction of identity from a young age. Fathers often instill ideas about self-worth, resilience, responsibility, and societal roles, guiding boys in how to channel their emotions and respond to challenges.

In a nurturing father-son relationship, boys are shown how to develop a sense of agency and responsibility. They learn essential lessons about empathy, the importance of integrity, and the need for introspection. Importantly, fathers model behaviors and attitudes that teach boys how to balance emotion with strength—integrating kindness, vulnerability, and assertiveness in ways that honor their unique identities. This guidance helps boys to understand their place in the world and how to express their masculinity positively.

However, for many Black boys, the experience of growing up without a father figure is a painful reality influenced by systemic inequalities that disproportionately affect Black families. High rates of incarceration, economic instability, and societal marginalization contribute to father absence, which can cause boys to grapple with confusion around their identities. They may mimic maternal behaviors out of necessity but may struggle to reconcile these approaches with societal expectations of masculinity, which are often rooted in traditional and hyper-masculine archetypes.

Coping Mechanisms and Behavioral Adaptations

In the face of father absence, Black boys often develop various coping mechanisms and behavioral adaptations, some of which can be detrimental to their overall emotional and psychological development.

1. **Mimicking Maternal Behavior:** In situations where Black boys lack paternal influence, they may unconsciously adopt their mothers' coping strategies. While mothers often embody nurturing and empathetic qualities, boys may find themselves in conflict as they seek to meet societal expectations of masculinity that emphasize toughness and emotional restraint. This conflict can lead to confusion about their own identities, causing them to oscillate between emotional expression and suppression.

2. **Hyper-Masculinity:** Some boys may respond to the absence of a father by adopting hyper-masculine traits as a means of compensating for what they perceive to be a lack in their upbringing. They may embrace aggression, emotional aloofness, or risk-taking behaviors to assert their manhood. Ironically, while such traits can provide a temporary sense of identity, they can also create barriers to forming healthy relationships and ultimately lead to destructive patterns of behavior.

3. **Substance Misuse and Risky Behaviors:** Boys lacking the guidance of a father may experiment with risky behaviors, including substance use, as a method of coping with emotional pain and seeking belonging. These behaviors often serve as maladaptive coping strategies that mask deeper issues related to abandonment, inadequacy, and anger. The allure of these unhealthy choices can create cycles of dependency and self-destruction, ultimately exacerbating their feelings of isolation and disconnection.

4. **Aggression and Disruptive Behavior:** Anger and frustration may manifest in boys as externalized behaviors. Without a father to model healthy emotional processing, some boys might express their grief through aggression, and acting out in school or at home. This can include bullying, defiance, and other disruptive behaviors intended to seek attention or assert dominance in social environments. Tragically, these actions can further alienate them from potential mentors or positive influences in their lives.

5. **Emotional Suppression:** An absence of paternal support can lead to emotional repression, where boys feel compelled to hide their vulnerabilities and grievances. In an effort to display toughness—whether as a means of self-preservation or in reaction to societal expectations—

they may avoid seeking help or expressing their emotions openly. This emotional suppression can contribute to mental health challenges such as depression, anxiety, and difficulty in forming intimate relationships.

Compounding Factors Influencing Self-Perception

The impact of father absence on Black boys' self-perception is further complicated by the intersection of various factors, making it a multi-faceted issue:

1. **Societal Narratives and Stereotypes:** The broader societal narratives surrounding masculinity often depict rigid archetypes—strength, dominance, emotional stoicism—that fail to account for the complexities of Black boyhood. When fathers are absent, boys may struggle to navigate these conflicting messages. The pressure to conform to these damaging stereotypes can lead to a disjointed sense of self, further reinforcing unhealthy behaviors and identities.

2. **Peer Influence:** In the absence of paternal guidance, Black boys often turn to peer groups for validation. While friendships can provide a sense of belonging, they can also reinforce negative expressions of masculinity. Peer pressures in their environments may encourage behaviors such as bullying or homophobia as means of proving themselves. This creates a cycle where boys feel they must assert their masculinity in aggressive or harmful ways to be accepted.

3. **Media Representation:** The portrayal of Black masculinity in media is often problematic, typifying Black men through lenses of violence, aggression, and emotional detachment. Boys without active father figures may internalize these portrayals, adopting them as templates for identity formation. Such distorted views can create unhealthy expectations about relationships and masculinity, further complicating their emotional landscape.

Pathways to Resiliency

Despite the myriad challenges arising from father absence, Black boys can still cultivate resilience and develop a positive story of self. Critical to this journey are the following pathways of support:

1. **Community Support:** Mentorship programs and community-based initiatives can serve as vital resources for Black boys seeking positive role models. Community leaders, coaches, and teachers can provide guidance and encouragement, helping them navigate their identities in healthier ways. Many programs exist to foster relationships that bridge the gap left by absent fathers, offering examples of what positive masculinity can look like.

2. **Cognitive Behavioral Theory:** Cognitive Behavioral Theory (CBT) emphasizes the relationship between thoughts, feelings, and behaviors, making it a powerful framework for helping boys navigate their identities. CBT-based programs can provide boys with essential tools to recognize and challenge negative thought patterns that may arise from the absence of a father figure. By learning to identify distorted thinking and replace it with more constructive beliefs, boys can enhance their self-esteem and improve their emotional responses to various situations. Through practical exercises and guided discussions, these programs encourage open communication and help boys develop problem-solving skills, ultimately fostering resilience as they face life's challenges.

3. **Empowering Education:** Educational institutions play a crucial role in shaping boys' self-perceptions. Curricula that tackle traditional notions of masculinity can dismantle harmful stereotypes and elevate diverse narratives of self-worth and identity. By encouraging discussions about vulnerability, emotional expression, and respect for others, classrooms can become spaces that prioritize mental well-being and healthy masculinity.

4. **Encouraging Positive Relationships:** Encouraging boys to foster relationships built on empathy and understanding can help them navigate their identities more smoothly. By cultivating spaces where boys learn to communicate, listen, and support each other, we can foster environments that prioritize emotional health and respect for diverse identities.

The absence of fathers, particularly within the context of Black communities, profoundly affects boys' self-perception and identity. The emotional, social, and psychological ramifications of growing up without a father figure create myriad challenges, ranging from feelings of abandonment to maladaptive coping mechanisms. However, amid these challenges lies the potential for growth and transformation.

By addressing the complexities of masculinity, especially as they pertain to the unique experiences of Black boys, we can identify ways to support their journeys toward healthier identities. As society continues to have conversations about masculinity and fatherhood, it is imperative to advocate for resources, programs, and structures that empower boys to cultivate positive senses of self. By rebuilding narratives around masculinity and fostering supportive environments, we pave the way for future generations of boys to grow into emotionally intelligent, resilient men who positively contribute to society.

Young Black Men's Struggles, Experiences and Resilience

The experiences of young Black men in America are multifaceted, shaped by the intersections of race, class, and gender. As they transition from boys to young men, many grapple with societal expectations, familial responsibilities, and systemic challenges. Throughout my journey of serving young Black boys and men, I have learned invaluable lessons about their struggles and triumphs, which serve to illuminate their voices and offer insights into their lived experiences.

The Impact of Father Absence

One of the most prominent challenges many young Black men face is the absence of a father figure. In my work with these young men, I have witnessed firsthand the heavy load this absence imposes on their identities. Many grow up in single-parent households and long for the guidance that a father might provide. I have heard stories of young boys yearning for male role models, reflecting a deep-seated desire to understand what it means to be a man.

This absence often leaves them feeling inadequate and confused about their emotional landscape. I've encountered young men who struggle with articulating their feelings, many battling feelings of anger and frustration that stem from a lack of paternal influence. I've seen how these feelings manifest in their interactions and relationships, often leading them to seek validation through negative or risky behaviors.

Societal Expectations and Peer Influence

As these young men grow older, they encounter societal expectations that define masculinity in restrictive terms. Many feel pressured to conform to stereotypical images of Black masculinity, which often paint them as tough or aggressive. In my conversations with them, I've learned how draining and disheartening it can be to wrestle with these expectations. I've seen the courage it takes for them to express their true identities in a world that often seeks to pigeonhole them.

I recall engaging with a young man who played sports and felt he had to maintain a tough exterior, suppressing anxieties that burdened him. It became evident how this facade can mask deeper struggles and inhibit their ability to express vulnerability. I've listened to stories that highlight a common theme: the fear of being perceived as weak often leads these young men to bottle up their emotions, creating a cycle of isolation.

The Role of Education and Systemic Barriers

Education serves as a critical arena for shaping the futures of young Black men, yet I often see how systemic barriers impede their progress. Many lack access to quality educational resources, and this inequality weighs heavily on their self-esteem and aspirations. While some of these young men have supportive figures in their lives—teachers, mentors, coaches—others face environments that seem stacked against them.

Through my work, I've come to understand the emotional toll that systemic inequality can exact. I have spoken with young men who share their fears about not belonging in academic settings, compounded by their experiences with police and societal discrimination. This duality—attending school during the day and fearing harassment in their neighborhoods—adds a layer of stress that is hard to navigate. Their stories reflect a deep yearning for affirmation and opportunities, underscoring the need for better support systems.

Navigating Relationships and Emotional Expression

Healthy emotional expression is a critical aspect of personal growth, yet young men often find themselves grappling with the societal stigma that discourages vulnerability. In my interactions with them, I've noted a recurring theme: many have been conditioned to view emotional expression as a sign of weakness. This belief can stunt their ability to process grief, sadness, and complex feelings.

I have listened to narratives of young men who feel the weight of expectations: to be strong for their families and communities, to be the protector. During my time with them, I've attempted to create safe spaces where they can share their experiences freely. It's inspiring to witness the transformation that occurs when they learn to express their emotions constructively. They explore avenues such as writing, art, and dialogue, using these mediums as tools for reflection and healing.

Resilience and the Search for Positive Role Models

One of the most heartening aspects of my service has been witnessing the incredible resilience among these young men. Many actively seek out positive role models, yearning for guidance that challenges traditional stereotypes. Mentorship programs can serve as beacons of hope, helping young men navigate the turbulent waters of adolescence and early adulthood.

I have seen the profound impact of mentorship on their lives. Many describe how having someone who believes in them can be life-changing, opening doors to internships, scholarships, and opportunities they never thought possible. These relationships provide not only guidance but also emotional support, helping them to redefine masculinity in a healthier, more inclusive way.

Family support also plays a crucial role in resilience. Many of the young men I've worked with draw strength from their mothers, recognizing the sacrifices made on their behalf. Their stories reflect a deep appreciation for maternal figures who encourage them to embrace their dreams, pushing back against the narrative of inadequacy that arises from father absence.

Celebrating Cultural Heritage

Amidst the struggles, the rich cultural heritage of the Black community emerges as a source of strength and pride. These young men often find empowerment in their history, community values, and shared experiences. They appreciate the music, art, and stories that shape their identities, drawing inspiration from those who have come before them.

Engaging with their cultural heritage can be a powerful act of reclamation. I've observed how the embrace of their identities fosters a sense of pride and belonging, encouraging them to write their own narratives rather than allowing society to define them. Creative expression becomes a powerful outlet, helping them navigate their complex emotions and experiences.

The stories and experiences of young Black men reflect a rich tapestry of resilience, struggle, and hope. Through my service to them, I've gained invaluable insights into the complexities they face daily. They navigate challenges stemming from father absence, societal expectations, and systemic barriers, all while seeking affirmation and support.

What stands out most is their unwavering resilience and drive to carve out their paths. Yet, they need our understanding, advocacy, and support to create environments where they can thrive. By amplifying their voices and recognizing their struggles, we can contribute to reshaping narratives surrounding Black masculinity, fostering a society where young Black men feel empowered to embrace their full selves.

The journey may be fraught with challenges, but the spirit of these young men remains unyielding, determined to rise above and pursue greatness. As I reflect on my experiences, I am inspired by their strength and reminded of the importance of creating spaces where they can flourish, ultimately encouraging a future defined not by limitations but by limitless possibilities.

The Shifts Towards More Feminine Expression in Young Black Men: The Nexus of Father Absence and Emotionality

The experiences of young Black men in contemporary society are complex and multifaceted, particularly concerning issues of identity, emotional expression, and masculinity. As sociocultural dynamics evolve, there has emerged a noticeable shift toward more feminine expressions in dress, behavior, and emotionality among some young Black men. This transformation can often be traced to the absence of positive father figures, which dramatically impact personal development, emotional health, and societal perceptions of masculinity.

In exploring this nexus, we will delve into how this shift in behavior may be both a reaction to systemic challenges and an attempt to create new definitions of masculinity. Furthermore, we will integrate biblical perspectives, particularly from the Scriptures, to highlight the importance of fatherhood and the emotional landscapes that God considers essential for human beings.

The Impact of Father Absence
The Societal Context

In many communities, particularly within Black families, the absence of fathers has reached alarming proportions. Statistics reveal that nearly 70% of Black children are born to single mothers, with absentee fathers leading to significant emotional and social ramifications for these youth. The direct impact of father absence has been linked to various behavioral problems, including issues with self-esteem, a higher likelihood of engaging in risky behavior, and struggles with emotional regulation.

A Gap in Role Models

Fathers often serve as role models for their children, especially in shaping concepts of masculinity. Young boys may look to their fathers to learn how to navigate their emotional worlds, understand relationships, and define their identities. In the absence of a father, these young men may not receive the necessary guidance on social interactions, emotional expression, or the complexities of adult life.

As children grow, they absorb the expectations and behaviors exhibited by those around them. When fathers are absent, alternative role models may emerge, but they may not embody the traditional traits associated with positive masculinity. Young Black men may find themselves influenced by media portrayals or the behaviors of peers, resulting in a skewed understanding of what it means to be "manly."

Differentiating Between Men and Women
Understanding Emotional Expression in Men and Boys

Expressions of emotion have traditionally been understood differently across genders. While emotional openness and genuine expression are crucial for everyone, how men and boys navigate these expressions can differ significantly from women and girls. Acknowledging these differences fosters an understanding of the unique experiences and challenges that young Black men face in their emotional journeys.

Redefining Masculinity

The conception of masculinity does not need to rely on stereotypes of stoicism or emotional suppression. Instead, it can encompass a rich array of emotional experiences that align with being a man. It is vital to embrace the idea that young Black men can express vulnerability and sensitivity without reshaping their identities into those traditionally associated with femininity.

Many young Black men are beginning to openly express their emotions while still retaining a distinct masculine identity. This evolution reflects a growing understanding that emotional strength is not synonymous with weakness, but rather a form of authenticity that enriches their character. Young men are learning that they can articulate their feelings in ways that are true to themselves while also being distinctly male.

Emotional Openness

The trend toward emotional openness is becoming increasingly prevalent among younger generations. As they navigate mental health issues, relationship dynamics, and personal struggles, many young men demonstrate a willingness to discuss their feelings in ways that are appropriate to their identities. This shift highlights the importance of connection and the need for a support system that fosters this kind of emotional sharing.

As stated in Proverbs 27:17, "Iron sharpens iron, and one man sharpens another." This scripture emphasizes the value of meaningful interaction among men, encouraging them to support one another in their emotional experiences. By creating environments where young Black men can express themselves genuinely, we nurture their ability to articulate feelings while maintaining their masculine essence.

Fashion and Identity

Shifts in fashion and appearance among young Black men have become increasingly noticeable, often reflecting broader cultural changes. While personal expression is important, there are concerns that some aspects of this expression may lean toward styles and behaviors that are perceived as more traditionally feminine. This trend can sometimes indicate an underlying struggle with identity and self-understanding, particularly in the absence of positive male role models.

The choices these young men make in clothing, grooming, and fashion can serve as both powerful indicators of self-identity and expressions of autonomy. However, without the guidance of father figures who embody healthy models of masculinity, young Black boys may struggle to find a balance in their self-expression. The lack of such mentorship can lead them to adopt styles that clash with traditional notions of manhood, resulting in a fashion sense that does not align with their intrinsic identity as men.

For men, we can reflect on the powerful words of 1 Corinthians 16:13-14 (ESV): "Be watchful, stand firm in the faith, act like men, be strong. Let all that you do be done in love." This scripture serves as a vital reminder for men to embody strength and vigilance while grounding their actions in love.

In the context of Black men and boys, the message takes on a deeper significance. True self-worth and confidence arise from understanding one's identity and purpose. In a society where many young Black men face external pressures and challenges that can distort their self-image, this understanding is crucial.

Without a foundation rooted in their God-given identity, young Black men may find themselves wandering toward expressions that embody confusion instead of clarity. They might seek validation through external means, such as societal approval or material possessions, rather than embracing their unique strengths and values.

This scripture encourages young Black men to find strength not just in external appearances, but in the core of who they are—individuals created with purpose and potential. By being vigilant in their faith and acting with love, they can cultivate a strong sense of self that empowers them to navigate life's challenges confidently and with integrity. In this way, they can inspire others and contribute positively to their communities, ultimately shaping a brighter future for themselves and those around them.

To foster a healthier sense of identity, it is essential to encourage mentorship and community support that guide young Black men in developing a self-expression that honors their masculinity while allowing them to be true to themselves. In doing so, we can help cultivate environments where emotional and fashion choices can coexist with a strong sense of manhood, ultimately empowering these young men to thrive.

Navigating Identity and Peer Influence

The absence of fathers can leave Black boys and young men to navigate the complex landscape of masculinity without guidance. In this void, peer groups often play a significant role in shaping their understanding of what it means to be a man today. While some peers may uphold traditional ideals of masculinity, others may challenge those norms, creating a spectrum of influences.

For many young men, the desire for acceptance within these peer groups can lead them to adopt behaviors that reflect their surroundings. In their search for connection, they might embrace traits and expressions that have historically been viewed as more feminine. While emotional expression is important for all individuals, it's crucial to recognize that aligning too closely with certain peer influences can sometimes steer young men away from traditional masculine ideals, which can affect their development and self-identity.

It is important for Black boys and young men to be discerning about who they identify with. By choosing role models and friends who embody positive aspects of masculinity—such as strength, integrity, and resilience—they can foster a sense of self that balances emotional depth with traditional masculine values. This mindful approach can help them cultivate strong, authentic relationships while ensuring they remain anchored in their identity as confident young men.

The Influence of Social Media on Masculinity

In today's digital age, social media significantly impacts how young men perceive and understand masculinity. They often look to influencers, celebrities, and online communities that highlight non-traditional expressions of manhood. While the visibility of diverse identities can empower young men to explore their individuality, it's essential to recognize that many of these public figures may not always serve as positive role models.

Too often, the lifestyles and messages propagated by certain celebrities can lead young Black men down paths that do not align with Yahweh's design for masculinity. This influence can create confusion about what it truly means to be a man. Thus, it is vital for young men to be discerning about whom they follow and draw inspiration from.

To cultivate a healthy understanding of masculinity and emotional expression, young men should seek out trustworthy figures who exemplify manhood as intended by God—marked by strength, integrity, and emotional depth. They should turn to mentors, family members, and community leaders who embody these qualities and can provide guidance rooted in biblical principles.

As stated in Proverbs 13:20 (NIV): *"Whoever walks with the wise becomes wise, but the companion of fools will suffer harm."* This verse highlights the significance of choosing one's companions wisely, reinforcing the idea that young Black men should seek out those who demonstrate positive and godly masculinity. By doing so, they can cultivate their identities in a way that aligns with Yahweh's intentions, avoiding the pitfalls that often come from following the wrong influences. This mindful approach will help them navigate the complexities of modern masculinity with clarity and confidence.

The Intersection of Culture and Faith
Exploring the Scriptures

At its core, faith plays an essential role in shaping how individuals view masculinity and emotional expression. Many biblical figures exemplify a range of emotional experiences—joy, grief, compassion, and anger—illustrating that feelings are a fundamental part of the human experience.

In the Book of Psalms, David openly expressed a wide spectrum of emotions, from deep sorrow to exuberant praise. This acknowledgment of vulnerability underscores that emotionality is part of the larger tapestry of faith. As we read in Psalm 34:18 (NIV), "The LORD is near to the brokenhearted and saves the crushed in spirit." This indicates that God values our emotional state and desires to be close to those who suffer.

Yahweh's Perspective on Fatherhood

In Hebrew culture, fatherhood is treated with immense responsibility and reverence. The role of a father is one of guidance, provision, and emotional support. The presence of a father creates a nurturing environment where young men can learn resilience, humility, and the importance of emotionality.

Yahweh Himself is often portrayed in the Scriptures as a paternal figure—compassionate, loving, and keenly aware of the struggles of His children. In Isaiah 64:8 (NIV), it is written, "But now, O LORD, you are our Father; we are the clay, and you are our potter; we are all the work of your hand." This verse emphasizes the importance of divine fatherhood and guidance, suggesting that a father's role is integral in shaping the lives of young people.

Addressing the Challenges: Healing and Restoration
The Need for Mentorship

The absence of fathers underscores the critical need for mentorship in communities. Our young Black boys and men require positive male figures to provide guidance, share experiences, and help them navigate their identities and emotions. Mentorship programs that connect youth with responsible male role models can bridge the gap created by father absence, instilling values that nurture healthy masculine identities.

Community Engagement and Support

Faith-based organizations can play a pivotal role in addressing these issues. They can provide safe spaces that foster discussions around masculinity and emotionality, where young men can express their feelings openly without fear of judgment. When churches and community groups embrace discussions on emotional well-being and promote healthy masculinity, they create environments that support emotional growth.

Encouraging Healthy Emotional Expression

Encouraging young Black men to embrace their full range of emotions is vital for mental health and well-being. Initiatives that focus on teaching young men how to articulate their feelings can transform their capacity for connection, ultimately benefiting their relationships. Incorporating scriptural teachings that promote emotional openness can help them understand that these expressions do not diminish their masculinity but rather enrich it.

Integrating Faith and Emotional Health

It is crucial to emphasize the connection between faith and emotional health, affirming that God desires His children, including young Black boys and men, to live full and thriving lives. Encouraging them to engage in prayer, meditation, and biblical study can be invaluable in helping them understand their emotions within a faith-based framework.

Scripture, such as Philippians 4:6-7 (NIV), provides profound insights: *"Do not be anxious about anything, but in everything by prayer and supplication with thanksgiving let your requests be made known to God. And the peace of God, which surpasses all understanding, will guard your hearts and your minds in Christ Jesus."* This verse underscores the significance of seeking divine guidance and assurance in times of emotional turmoil.

The shifts toward more expressive forms of dress, behavior, and emotionality among young Black men often reflect a complex response to modern masculinity, shaped in part by the absence of fathers. While these changes may raise eyebrows or invite criticism from traditionalists, it is essential to recognize that they arise from a genuine quest for authenticity, emotional connection, and healing.

In the context of father absence, the importance of positive male role models becomes even more apparent. Black boys and men must redirect their energies toward figures who can help them navigate their emotions healthily, without straying from God's design for masculinity. By embracing mentorship, community support, and spiritual guidance, we create avenues for healing and self-discovery, enabling young men to flourish.

Yahweh's vision for humanity includes a comprehensive view of masculinity, where emotional expression and strength can coexist harmoniously. By grounding ourselves in Scripture and integrating its teachings with practical support systems, we can foster a cultural shift that empowers young Black men to express their emotions while redefining masculinity in a way that aligns with God's requirements.

Recognizing and embracing their unique challenges can lead to a future where vulnerability is not seen as a weakness but celebrated as a strength. Each step toward understanding and acceptance brings us closer to a society where young Black men can thrive, fully embracing both their emotional truths and their dignity, fulfilling their roles as men in every sense of the word.

CHAPTER 4
RELATIONSHIPS AND INTERPERSONAL DYNAMICS

The impact of father absence within the Black community cannot be overstated; it reverberates through various aspects of life, profoundly influencing relationships and interpersonal dynamics, particularly in romantic contexts. This chapter delves into how the absence of fathers shapes the expectations and experiences of Black men and boys in their romantic relationships. It is not merely a question of missing a parental figure but rather one that influences identity formation, emotional health, and societal perceptions of Black masculinity.

For Black boys growing up without a father, the void left by paternal absence often leads to skewed understandings of love, intimacy, and partnership. As they mature into adulthood, these early impressions morph into expectations that dictate how they engage with women and perceive themselves in relationships. This chapter will explore these complex dynamics—how young Black men learn about love, loyalty, and masculinity in environments often devoid of positive male role models. By examining these experiences, we can better understand the multifaceted relationships that exist within the Black community and the ripple effects that father absence can have on romantic relationships.

The Impact of Father Absence on Expectations in Romantic Relationships
Understanding Masculinity in the Absence of Fathers

The absence of fathers significantly alters a young Black boy's understanding of masculinity. Without a paternal figure to model healthy masculine traits, boys may turn to alternative influences—media, peers, and societal stereotypes—to shape their perceptions of what it means to be a man. In a culture that often emphasizes hypermasculinity and emotional stoicism, young Black men may internalize the notion that expressing vulnerability equates to weakness.

Consequently, when they enter romantic relationships, these skewed ideas about masculinity can lead to difficulties in emotional expression and intimacy. Black men may struggle to communicate their feelings or rely heavily on defensive mechanisms, which can create barriers to genuine connection with their partners. These relational challenges contribute to unrealistic expectations, such as viewing love through a lens of ownership or control rather than mutual respect and collaboration.

The Role of Emotional Understanding

A strong grasp of feelings and interpersonal dynamics is vital for healthy relationships. Unfortunately, many young Black men, especially those raised without a father, often lack this understanding. I've witnessed firsthand how father absence can create a void that leaves these young men without guidance on positive emotional expression and conflict resolution.

One friend, for instance, found himself in a tumultuous relationship where he constantly clashed with his partner's family and friends. Lacking the communication skills to navigate those tensions, he often reacted defensively. I remember a heated argument escalating into violence—it began with an alleged slight, but before long, it involved shouting matches and physical confrontations. The fallout was devastating; not only did this alter his life trajectory, but it also left a lasting impression on everyone involved. It serves as a tragic illustration of how the inability to communicate effectively can lead to aggression and conflict.

In another instance, a young man I knew struggled with feelings of inadequacy and jealousy in his relationship. He would often assume that his partner should understand what he was going through without him needing to express it. When he perceived a lack of attention from her, his frustration grew until it culminated in a reckless act of aggression. This moment of impulsivity landed him in legal trouble and ultimately resulted in prison time. He often reflected on that moment, acknowledging that he didn't have the tools to express his emotions adequately.

Substance abuse can also be a consequence of this emotional gap. I've seen young men turn to drugs as a coping mechanism when faced with the pressures and hurt stemming from their relationships. One acquaintance fell into a cycle of addiction, initially using drugs to escape feelings of inadequacy and heartbreak. Each relationship he entered mirrored the last, fraught with miscommunication and conflict, leading him deeper into substance use. His struggle with mental health issues spiraled as he became more isolated, believing that the cycles of violence and heartache were part of an inevitable pattern.

The stories of these young men serve to illustrate a broader reality: when emotional understanding is absent, the results can be catastrophic. The inability to identify, articulate, or confront feelings can lead to misunderstandings that fester, culminating in violent outbursts or destructive behaviors. Furthermore, without a solid foundation for emotional health, many young Black men find themselves battling not only interpersonal conflicts but also the demons of mental and behavioral health issues as they navigate the complexities of their relationships.

The absence of a father not only deprives them of essential life lessons but also sets off a chain reaction that impacts their relationships and futures. We must address these gaps to prevent the cycle of dysfunction, violence, and emotional turmoil that too many young Black men experience. Only by fostering an environment where emotional understanding can thrive can we hope to alter the course of these young lives.

Learning Relationships Through Observation

For many young Black men, their observations of relationships among friends, family members, or in the media become their guide. Without a father to demonstrate healthy interactions, these boys often witness dysfunctional patterns—such as infidelity, emotional detachment, or toxic masculinity—during formative years. This environment can create a desensitization toward unhealthy relationship dynamics, leading them to accept subpar treatment from partners or perpetuate cycles of dysfunction.

Many young Black men grow up absorbing societal messages that equate love and respect with material wealth, status, or physical attraction. This conditioning influences how they approach relationships, often leading to a transactional view where the worth of a connection is measured by what one can offer materially rather than emotionally or spiritually.

I recall a time when a friend was deeply infatuated with the idea of "making it big." His notion of success was intertwined with the acquisition of flashy cars and designer clothes. In pursuit of this lifestyle, he sought quick financial gains through illegal means. He believed that these symbols of success would attract the right kind of partner—someone who could appreciate and validate his newfound status. Unfortunately, this misalignment of values led him to relationships characterized by superficiality. His partners were often drawn to his possessions rather than his character, and while the initial attraction may have felt exhilarating, it quickly devolved into emptiness and dissatisfaction.

Similar stories abound among his peers. One young man I knew thought that being "the man" meant flaunting wealth through extravagant spending and hosting lavish parties. In his eyes, this was how he would attract loyalty and admiration from his friends and potential partners. However, when the money ran out, so did the friends. They were less interested in the person behind the facade, leaving him feeling isolated and disillusioned. He now struggles to form genuine connections, constantly questioning why he can't find people who embrace him for who he truly is, not just what he can provide.

This fixation on materialism also leads many young men down dangerous paths. I remember another acquaintance who resorted to drug dealing as a means to achieve the lifestyle he believed would earn him respect. He thought that by accumulating cash and presenting himself as a "big shot," he would solidify his status among peers and attract attention from women. In the end, his choices led to legal troubles and lost opportunities. The relationships he built during that time were unstable and often exploitative, leaving him to grapple with loneliness and regret when the thrill of the lifestyle faded.

The real tragedy is that many of these young men haven't taken the time to discover who they are beyond societal expectations. The pursuit of material gain clouds their understanding of their own identity and purpose. They need to recognize that to draw in fulfilling relationships, they must first be grounded in self-awareness and authenticity. The truth is, building a life based on productivity, consistency, and ambition fosters a more meaningful connection to others.

Those who take the time to cultivate their goals, understand their values, and invest in their personal growth often find that the right partners are naturally drawn to them. When individuals know who they are, they can better navigate the complexities of connections, seeking out relationships that are enriching rather than transactional.

By shifting the focus from superficial markers of success to genuine self-discovery, young Black men can break free from the cycle of pursuing validation through materialism. When they embrace their true selves, they can create bonds rooted in mutual respect, shared values, and emotional depth—qualities that will ultimately foster lasting and meaningful relationships. The journey of self-discovery is one of the most important paths they can take, leading not only to personal growth but also to richer, more satisfying connections with others.

Navigating Stereotypes and Pressure in Romantic Contexts

The societal expectations placed on Black men can exacerbate the challenges they face in romantic relationships. Stereotypes often label Black men as hypersexual, emotionally unavailable, or aggressive, contributing to an internalized pressure to perform within these constrained identities. This pressure can lead them to act out in ways that reinforce those stereotypes, creating a self-fulfilling prophecy.

As a result, young Black men may feel compelled to outwardly demonstrate their masculinity in romantic situations, neglecting personal desires in favor of conforming to societal roles that dictate how they should act or feel. This can lead to precarious relationships built on assumptions rather than mutual understanding and respect.

The Importance of Positive Male Role Models

While father absence poses considerable challenges, the presence of other positive male role models can have a transformative impact on young Black men's relationship expectations. Mentorship programs, community organizations, or simply strong male figures in their lives can teach young men about compassion, respect, and the importance of emotionality in relationships.

These role models can provide essential guidance in forming healthy romantic relationships. Through their experiences, young Black men can learn resilience, the art of effective communication, and emotional openness, which help to dismantle harmful stereotypes while fostering deeper connections with partners.

Redefining Expectations through Faith and Community Support

Integrating faith into discussions of relationships may provide an additional layer of support for Black men seeking to navigate their romantic lives. Faith communities often promote values of love, respect, and commitment—ideals that can seem unattainable in a world rife with negative stereotypes. Engaging in faith-based activities, such as group discussions or workshops, allows young men to explore their identities in a context that encourages healthy emotional expression and mutual support.

Community support expands their networks, creating spaces for constructive dialogue and shared experiences. Through such connections, young Black men can gain insight into what healthy romantic relationships look like, helping them redefine their expectations based on values instilled by both personal and collective experiences.

The Journey Towards Healing and Growth

Ultimately, understanding the impacts of father absence on expectations in romantic relationships involves acknowledging the broader context of healing and growth. Young Black men must confront their struggles, redefine their notions of masculinity, and learn to embrace vulnerability as a source of strength.

By participating in group discussions, therapy, or mentorship initiatives, they can cultivate emotional literacy, foster vulnerability, and work toward breaking cycles of dysfunction that influence their romantic endeavors. As they gain insight into their emotions and expectations, they will increasingly draw from a well-rounded, healthy perspective on love—transforming not only their relationships but also their lives.

The absence of fathers has far-reaching effects on young Black men, particularly in the realm of romantic relationships. Understanding how this absence shapes their expectations—through skewed perceptions of masculinity, emotional challenges, societal pressures, and the necessity of positive role models—provides valuable insight into their interpersonal dynamics.

By prioritizing emotional health, deepening connections through faith and community support, and embracing personal growth and healing, members of the Black community can cultivate healthier and richer romantic relationships. Ultimately, the journey toward transforming expectations and experiences in love begins with a commitment to understanding, acknowledging, and reshaping the narratives surrounding the experience of father absence.

Dependency, Emotional Labor, and Communication Styles
The Impact of Father Absence

In numerous conversations with young Black men, I often find myself reflecting on a recurring theme: the absence of fathers and its profound impact on their emotional development, communication styles, and relationship dynamics. The issues of dependency, emotional labor, and communication styles are intricately tied to this absence, raising the pressing question—where's your daddy?

The Role of Fathers in Emotional Development

Numerous studies reveal that fathers play a crucial role in the emotional and social development of their children. According to a report by the U.S. Department of Health and Human Services, children who grow up without a father are at a higher risk for encounters with behavioral problems, psychological issues, and struggles in forming healthy relationships (U.S. DHHS, 2017). Without a father figure, young men often lack models for emotional expression and conflict resolution, leading to difficulties in handling their feelings and forming healthy attachments.

I can recall several instances that illustrate this theme vividly. One friend struggled significantly with emotional dependency—he often clung to relationships, looking for validation through partners. Without a father to imitate, he relied on those around him to instill a sense of self-worth. His pursuit of approval became a pattern in every relationship, often leading to heart-wrenching disappointments. He would pour emotional labor into relationships without receiving support in return, leaving him feeling drained and confused.

The absence of a father also contributed to unhealthy patterns of communication. In our conversations, I would notice how he hesitated to express vulnerability. When his partner would ask about his feelings, he often deflected or made jokes—anything but a direct response. This evasion created barriers in his relationships, reinforcing cycles of miscommunication and frustration. Ultimately, I couldn't help but think: where's your daddy? Where were the lessons about emotional honesty that could have shaped how he approached intimacy and vulnerability?

Dependency and Emotional Labor

Dependency is a double-edged sword. On one hand, it reflects the innate human need for connection, but when it is unbalanced, it can manifest as toxic dependency. Many young Black men, having grown up without consistent paternal figures, may rely heavily on romantic partners for emotional support. This reliance often leads to one person taking on the emotional labor in the relationship—managing feelings, resolving conflicts, and providing reassurance—while the other may remain emotionally absent or disengaged.

I remember talking with another close acquaintance who found himself in a cycle of relationships where he bore the burden of emotional labor. He would reassure partners constantly, but when it came time for him to express his own feelings, they fell on deaf ears. The frustration of trying to be the emotional anchor while receiving little in return eroded his self-esteem. Over time, he began to equate love with sacrifice and neglected his own needs. The question loomed again: where's your daddy? Where was the guidance that would help him navigate the complexities of emotional exchange and mutual support?

Communication Styles and The Void of Fatherly Guidance

Communication styles are often developed through observation and experience, particularly with parental figures. In households where fathers are absent, young Black men may struggle to learn how to approach conflict, express vulnerability, and articulate their needs. This lack of skill perpetuates patterns of maladaptive communication, including avoidance, aggression, or passive-aggressive behavior.

In one instance, a young man I knew had difficulty addressing problems directly. Instead of discussing conflicts openly, he would resort to cold shoulders and silence. This often left his partners feeling frustrated and bewildered, as they couldn't decipher what was wrong. When I gently probed him about his upbringing, I discovered that he had grown up watching his mother navigate challenges alone. In his mind, vulnerability was a weakness—an idea that might have been a protective measure taught by a father who was never present to model emotional discussions. The emotional labor involved in this kind of communication left him feeling alienated and misunderstood.

Research supports this notion, as studies show that absent fathers contribute to the development of avoidant or anxious attachment styles, which directly impact one's ability to connect and communicate effectively in relationships (Bowlby, 1982). The correlations are evident—not only in personal stories but also in emotional theory. By lacking the foundational guidance of a father figure, these young men often resort to unhealthy coping mechanisms, hindering their ability to foster deep connections, further raising the question: where's your daddy?

The Importance of Healthy Relationships with Yahweh

While the absence of a father can leave gaping wounds, I've also seen that a relationship with Yahweh can serve as a transformative force in reclaiming emotional health and building meaningful connections. A spiritual foundation equips young Black men with hope, direction, and a sense of purpose—qualities that can mitigate the impact of father absence.

During my own journey, I found solace and empowerment in my relationship with Yahweh. In seeking guidance through prayer and scripture, I began to understand the significance of self-worth beyond materialism or human validation. When I shared my experiences with those around me, several young men resonated with the idea that a spiritual connection provided them with something they had lacked—unconditional love, acceptance, and guidance.

One young man I met boldly claimed his faith as a source of strength after grappling with painful relationships. He reflected that turning to Yahweh helped him redefine his self-worth. This newfound spiritual connection fostered a deeper understanding of love that wasn't transactional, and it illuminated the importance of being rooted in something greater—a far cry from the dependency he had often experienced.

Moreover, through prayer and introspection, he learned to value open, honest communication—both with himself and with others. He began to approach relationships with a sense of purpose and clarity, breaking free from cycles of emotional labor that had defined his past connections. He found strength in expressing vulnerability, which in turn brought about healthier, more meaningful relationships.

Engaging with Yahweh not only helped him confront his dependency issues but also guided him toward emotional maturity. He began to see relationships as collaborations rather than transactions, paving the way for deeper emotional connections that mirrored the love he had found in his spirituality.

Building a Legacy for Future Generations

Through these stories, we can see how essential the role of a father—or a father figure—can be in a young man's life. We must address the issue of father absence head-on, advocating for fathers to step up and show up in their children's lives. Moreover, we can't overlook the critical role of spiritual relationships in mediating some of these deficits.

As we reflect upon these challenges—dependency, emotional labor, and communication—we recognize that the journey does not end here. There's hope for change and growth. By equipping young Black men with the tools to build a relationship with Yahweh, we promote healing and resilience. The challenge lies in fostering environments that encourage self-exploration, emotional honesty, and open communication.

We can inspire the next generation to break the cycle of father absence through intentional fatherhood or mentorship programs that teach emotional intelligence. It's imperative for young men to wield their dependency not as a crutch but as a motivator for self-discovery and growth.

Ultimately, when I see these young men grappling with issues of dependency or emotional labor, I will continue to ask, where's your daddy? I do so not as a judgment, but as a reflection—prompting them to research their backgrounds, recognize their emotional struggles, and consider their relationships with both their fathers and Yahweh. This awareness can empower them to become who they were meant to be, fostering a generation of emotionally competent, spiritually grounded individuals capable of forming meaningful connections.

The intertwining issues of dependency, emotional labor, and communication styles require a concerted effort to address the implications of father absence among young Black men. By examining their stories, we uncover the deep-seated patterns of emotional struggle and relational challenges. However, the transformative power of faith, mentorship, and self-awareness offers a beacon of hope. As we advocate for healthier relationships and encourage meaningful self-exploration, we can help these young men reframe their narratives, cultivate a deeper understanding of love, and build connections rooted in mutual respect and emotional resilience.

Navigating Partnership Roles Through the Absence of Black Fathers

The absence of Black fathers presents a profound challenge for young men, shaping their understanding of partnership roles and the dynamics of relationships. In a society where a father's presence is instrumental in modeling healthy emotional and relational behaviors, the fallout from this absence can lead to significant gaps in understanding intimacy, responsibility, and emotional intelligence. These challenges are especially pronounced in the context of healthy partnerships, where young men might struggle to navigate their roles without a father figure to guide them.

The Impact of Father Absence

The impact of father absence is multifaceted, affecting young men's self-esteem, identity, and relational skills. Research indicates that children who grow up without fathers often face a higher risk of developing behavioral issues and forming unhealthy relationships (Martin, 2020). Emotional intelligence—a critical component in understanding and engaging in partnerships—is often lacking. This void can lead to an array of challenges in how young men interact with romantic partners, friends, and family members.

In conversations with young men who grew up in father-absent households, many express feelings of confusion regarding their role in relationships. One story that strikes me is that of a young man I met who found himself caught in a cycle of short-lived relationships. He described feeling lost when it came to understanding what was expected of him in a partnership. "It's like I'm pretending to know what I'm doing, but inside, I'm just as lost as I was before," he shared, reflecting a deeper truth that resonates with many young Black men in similar situations.

The absence of a father, particularly in the formative years, often leads to a lack of models for healthy relationships—both romantic and platonic. With many role models absent, these young men may resort to media portrayals or peer examples that reinforce negative stereotypes of masculinity and partnership. This creates an environment where uncertainty and misinformation flourish, leaving them ill-equipped for the challenges of adult relationships.

The Challenges of Partnership Roles

In navigating partnership roles, young men without fathers frequently find themselves facing unique stresses and misconceptions about masculinity and relationships. The influence of societal expectations can create a sense of pressure that complicates their ability to connect with others.

One young man recounted an experience of trying to impress a romantic partner by adopting behaviors he believed were expected of him. He invested heavily in material displays of affection—lavishing gifts and attempting grand gestures—only to feel empty when his efforts did not result in lasting connections. "I used to think that's what love was," he explained. "But it just felt like I was trying to fill a void in a way that didn't matter." He eventually realized that the foundation of a healthy partnership extends far beyond superficial offerings. It requires genuine emotional engagement and understanding—areas where he felt his father's absence was deeply felt.

The difficulty of understanding partnership roles might also manifest as a fear of vulnerability. Many young men share that they grapple with the idea of expressing feelings openly—fearing judgment or rejection. In a world where vulnerability is often misconstrued as weakness, the absence of a father figure to model emotional openness can hinder their ability to communicate effectively with partners. Another young friend described how he often resorted to humor or anger instead of sharing what he was feeling. "It's like I'm stuck," he confessed. "I want to tell her I care, but it's hard to let down my guard. I feel like I'd be exposing a part of myself that I don't even understand yet."

The inability to articulate emotions and navigate vulnerability can create significant barriers in relationships, leading to misunderstandings and conflicts. This cycle can perpetuate feelings of inadequacy and loneliness— feeding the narrative that relationships are inherently fraught with difficulty.

Teaching Healthy Partnership Roles

To break the cycle of father absence, it is crucial to create spaces where young men can learn about healthy partnership dynamics and emotional intelligence. Intentional fatherhood programs and mentorship initiatives can play a transformative role in equipping young Black men with the skills they need to navigate relationships confidently.

One impactful program I encountered partnered young men with mentors who filled the role of positive father figures. These mentors guided discussions about healthy relationships, emphasizing the importance of respect, communication, and accountability. In one session, several participants shared their experiences with conflict in relationships. One young man, previously hesitant to voice his feelings, found himself opening up about how fear of rejection hindered his emotional expression.

"I realized that the way I communicated with her was lacking because I didn't understand that not being perfect was okay," he noted. "Learning that it's human to mess up helped me see things differently. I felt like I could actually be myself, flaws and all." The ability to share and hear experiences fostered a sense of solidarity and empowerment among participants, ultimately reinforcing the idea that partnership is a shared journey.

The mentors guided these young men through various scenarios in which they could practice effective communication skills, empathy, and emotional regulation. These exercises not only illuminated the importance of emotional intelligence in relationships but also provided tangible tools for navigating the complexities of partnership roles.

Furthermore, an awareness of cultural values and the historical context surrounding Black fatherhood can support program participants as they navigate relationships. Addressing the systemic challenges that contribute to father absence—including economic disparities, mass incarceration, and socio-political factors—helps young men recognize they are part of a broader narrative that impacts their experiences. Awareness can foster resilience and a commitment to breaking generational cycles.

The Role of Community in Healing

Community plays a vital role in addressing the consequences of father absence. Support networks that celebrate fatherhood and positive male role models can help cultivate a culture that values emotional intelligence and healthy partnership dynamics. Encouraging community engagement can foster supportive relationships among young men who may be navigating similar challenges.

An example of this in action is a local church group focused on mentorship and support for young Black men. They created safe spaces where young men could voice their struggles and experiences, receiving guidance and advice from older male figures. In these discussions, mentors emphasized that a father's role is not limited to biological ties; their presence in young men's lives could come through mentorship, guidance, and love.

In one session, a young man shared his struggles with commitment. He admitted that observing the relationships around him—particularly those of his mother, who had raised him alone—fostered a fear of intimacy. He learned from mentors to confront those fears, understand their roots, and approach relationships more openly. "I never really thought about how much my past affected how I saw love," he reflected. "Talking about it made it easier to face my feelings, to understand that commitment doesn't equal losing myself."

Through community support and mentorship, young men are empowered to challenge their assumptions about partnership roles, emotional expression, and vulnerability. The potential for growth lies not only in personal development but also in the relationships forged through these interactions, fostering a cultural legacy that encourages healthy masculinity and emotional intelligence.

Creating a Legacy of Presence

To address the absent fathers in our communities, we must prioritize a legacy of presence, demonstrating that fatherhood encompasses mentorship, guidance, and leadership. Encouraging responsible male figures to engage in the lives of young men highlights the profound impact of having stable, supportive relationships. By modeling healthy partnership behaviors, mentors can help young men better understand their roles and responsibilities in relationships.

For example, positive role models can emphasize elements such as communication, respect, and emotional sharing, fleshing out what a nurturing partnership looks like. As one mentor recounted his experiences, he noted the value of demonstrating vulnerability to the young men he mentored; by allowing them to witness his own struggles and fears, he reinforced that it is acceptable to be imperfect and open.

These lessons can then ripple through the generations, creating environments where emotional intelligence becomes a foundational component of relationship dynamics. Young men who experience positive mentorship can internalize values of respect, empathy, and open communication, paving the way for healthier partnerships in their adult lives.

The key lies in intentionality—both in the actions of mentors and the structures that support their efforts. Communities can reinforce these values by highlighting and celebrating the positive impact of fathers, not limited to biological ones. Workshops, community events, and support groups focused on partnership skills can foster environments where young men feel empowered to acknowledge and challenge the effects of father absence in their lives.

The absence of Black fathers presents numerous challenges to young men as they navigate partnership roles in a complex world. The lack of fatherly guidance can lead to confusion regarding emotional intelligence, communication, and relationship dynamics. However, a commitment to mentorship, community support, and intentional fatherhood can create positive change.

By fostering environments where young men can explore their emotions, learn about healthy relationships, and engage with positive role models, we can break harmful cycles and build a legacy that values emotional depth, vulnerability, and partnership. Such efforts are crucial for equipping future generations with the necessary tools to thrive in their relationships and cultivate emotional intelligence.

As we address the pressing issue of father absence and its far-reaching consequences, let us remember the transformative power of connection, understanding, and a commitment to ensuring no young man has to navigate these challenges alone. Through mentorship and community, we can empower the next generation to embrace their roles in partnerships boldly and wisely, creating a healthier, more emotionally intelligent future.

CHAPTER 5
REASSERTING MASCULINITY IN LEADERSHIP

In today's society, the image of Black masculinity is being reshaped, often in ways that evoke concern and debate. As I observe young Black men in the church, the very fabric of our community seems to be fraying. Many of these young men have adopted styles that blur the lines of gender identity—wearing tights that evoke femininity, dancing in manners seen as traditionally feminine, and sporting hairstyles that defy cultural norms for masculinity. This phenomenon is alarming and raises important questions about the influence of contemporary culture on our youth and their understanding of what it means to be a man.

The church, long considered a pillar of strength and guidance within the Black community, should serve as the foundation for masculine leadership. However, as these young men mirror the world's trends, they risk losing not only their identity but also the opportunity to occupy positions of leadership that can inspire others. 1 Corinthians 11:4 (NIV) teaches, "Every man who prays or prophesies with his head covered dishonors his head." This scripture emphasizes the need for men to embrace their roles with honor and distinction. It's imperative that we recognize the potential consequences of a generation that is increasingly disconnected from traditional ideals of masculinity.

Moreover, 1 Corinthians 11:14 (NIV) reminds us, "Does not nature itself teach you that if a man wears long hair it is a disgrace for him?" This is not merely about hair length; it symbolizes a deeper crisis of identity and the erosion of boundaries that define male leadership. As these expressions become more mainstream, we must consider the message they send, not only to our peers but to younger generations yearning for guidance.

Addressing the presence of effeminate expressions among Black men in the church is a critical concern that intersects with scriptural teachings and Christian traditions. As highlighted in 1 Corinthians 6:9 (KJV), the Apostle Paul explicitly warns that "neither fornicators, nor idolaters, nor adulterers, nor effeminate" will inherit the kingdom of God. This verse reflects a long-standing biblical understanding of masculinity that prioritizes distinct gender roles and behaviors. When church members embrace styles or behaviors that blur these lines, it not only contradicts scriptural mandates but also undermines the church's role as a bastion of moral guidance and traditional values. Upholding a standard of masculinity rooted in scripture is essential for fostering a community grounded in righteousness, enabling men to exemplify the strength and leadership that God calls them to embody within the faith.

In this chapter, we will explore the significance of reasserting a clear and positive representation of masculinity within the Black community. Strong male leadership must begin in our places of worship, where values are taught and modeled. It is within the church that we can cultivate a generation of leaders who embody resilience, responsibility, and respect. As we navigate the challenges posed by changing cultural norms, we must strive to restore the distinction of Black male leadership, ensuring that it remains a source of strength, pride, and inspiration for all.

The Need for Strong Male Role Models

The absence of strong male role models in the Black community poses a significant challenge, particularly within the church. Historically, the church has served as a cornerstone for social, spiritual, and moral development, and it has traditionally been a space where men could affirm and express their masculinity positively. However, contemporary trends show that Black men are increasingly absent from these spaces. The attendance patterns of Black women and men in religious services reveal a notable disparity, with Black women consistently demonstrating a higher level of participation. According to recent data, 52% of Black women attend religious services at least once a week (Pew Research Center, 2014). This commitment to regular worship highlights the significant role that faith and community play in the lives of Black women, providing them with spiritual support and a collective identity.

In contrast, Black men exhibit a concerning trend regarding church attendance. Despite historically being a major demographic in the Black Church—a cornerstone of community life and a source of belonging—there has been a significant decline in attendance among Black men. Estimates suggest that 70-80% of Black men do not attend church services, whether in person or online (Hoffman, 2019). This trend is particularly troubling, given that over 80% of those who do not attend still consider themselves religious and believe in a higher power. This disconnect raises important questions regarding the factors influencing church participation among Black men and the implications for community cohesion and spiritual health.

The persistent attendance gap between Black women and men highlights the need for a deeper understanding of the cultural, social, and psychological factors that contribute to this phenomenon. Addressing the reasons behind the decline in Black men's church attendance is essential not only for fostering spiritual engagement but also for strengthening community bonds that have historically been anchored in the church. This disparity highlights a concerning reality: as Black women become increasingly visible and active in church settings, the male presence, particularly that of fathers and mentors, diminishes.

The critical role of father figures and mentors in shaping the identities of young Black boys cannot be overstated. Research indicates that positive male role models are essential for developing a healthy understanding of masculinity. According to a study conducted by the Child Trends organization, boys who grow up in father-absent homes are **twice as likely** to drop out of school, **four times more likely** to be in poverty, and **more likely** to engage in criminal behavior (Child Trends, 2019). The absence of these figures can lead to confusion about masculinity, often resulting in young men mimicking harmful stereotypes or embracing behaviors counterproductive to their well-being.

Furthermore, the lack of recognizable male leadership in the church contributes to this crisis. Without strong, positive role models, young Black men are left to navigate their identities in a world that increasingly challenges traditional notions of masculinity. In the absence of guiding figures, many may gravitate towards alternative influences that echo the values found in popular culture, which often perpetuates toxic masculinity, violence, and emotional suppression.

When churches actively engage in creating mentorship opportunities and involve male leaders in nurturing relationships, they foster environments that promote positive identity formation and responsible leadership.

By reasserting the presence of strong male role models within the church, we can provide young Black boys with the guidance they need to navigate their identities with confidence and integrity. This effort is crucial not only for individual development but also for the broader health of the community, as strong male leadership can inspire collective action, resilience, and a renewed commitment to the values that uphold our families and churches. As we address the crisis of absent fathers and male role models, the church has a unique opportunity to lead the charge in redefining masculinity in a manner that is constructive, nurturing, and rooted in faith.

Defining Traditional Masculinity

In contemporary discourse, the concept of masculinity is undergoing significant re-evaluation, often leading to the questioning of longstanding traditions. However, as articulated in 2 Thessalonians 2:15 (NKJV), "Therefore, brethren, stand fast and hold the traditions which you were taught, whether by word or our epistle," there is profound value in upholding certain time-honored principles, particularly those associated with traditional masculinity. Embodying traditional masculinity does not mean clinging to antiquated stereotypes, but rather embracing characteristics such as strength, responsibility, and leadership in a way that fosters community and personal growth.

Traditional masculinity can be defined positively through the lens of responsibility and moral integrity. Strength is not merely physical; it also encompasses emotional fortitude, reliability, and the capacity to endure challenges, providing a solid foundation for others to lean upon. Responsible men take ownership of their actions and consequences, creating a sense of trust within families and communities. Leadership, too, is vital—it involves guiding others not through force or dominance, but by inspiring and nurturing them towards collective goals. These qualities contribute to a sense of stability and security that is essential for the healthy development of individuals and communities alike.

An illustrative story can highlight the impact of traditional masculinity in fostering community. In a neighborhood that was facing rising levels of discontent and disarray, a man, known for his unwavering dependability, decided to spearhead a community initiative. He gathered a group of young men, many of whom had been struggling with uncertainty about their roles and futures. Through a series of meetings, he not only taught them practical skills—like budgeting, communication, and conflict resolution—but also shared his stories of overcoming personal difficulties.

His approach was not to impose his views but to model what it means to be a responsible man—one who is willing to engage, support, and uplift those around him. Over time, the group began to bond, fostering an environment where everyone felt valued and empowered. The young men learned not only the importance of hard work and resilience but also the significance of looking out for one another, reinforcing the values of commitment and leadership that are at the heart of traditional masculinity.

This man's initiative not only sparked growth among the youth but also revitalized a sense of community pride. Families began to come together, stronger and more cohesive, inspired by the leadership of someone who exemplified the values of traditional masculinity. His deeds resonated through the neighborhood, becoming a reminder of how fostering such values can lead to upliftment and positive change.

In anchoring ourselves to traditions that promote these principles, we cultivate a strong, resilient community capable of facing adversity together. By standing fast in such teachings, we ensure that the next generation has the guidance and role models needed to navigate life's challenges, ultimately leading to a healthier and more vibrant society. Thus, while it is crucial to adapt our understanding of masculinity to contemporary contexts, the foundational values of strength, responsibility, and leadership should not be abandoned but rather refined and celebrated for their role in empowering individuals and communities.

The Impact of Leadership Styles

Leadership within the Black community has undergone a significant transformation over recent decades, influenced by various cultural, social, and political factors. While historically, the Black church provided a sanctuary for spiritual leadership that emphasized morality, community uplift, and ethical guidance, contemporary leadership styles have increasingly diverged from this framework. As political engagement rises, some leaders, such as Rev. Al Sharpton, have expanded their platforms to encompass activism within political realms. This shift can sometimes dilute the traditional values of pastoral leadership, leading to a muddied understanding of what effective leadership looks like within the Black community.

Rev. Al Sharpton, once recognized primarily as a minister and civil rights activist, has become a prominent political figure. His involvement in politics has included commentary on national issues, often aligning with various political agendas rather than providing a strictly moral or spiritual compass. For instance, his transformation from a leader in the church to a political commentator exemplifies this shift. In my observation, Sharpton's work seems to straddle the line between spiritual leadership and political advocacy. This blending can sometimes create confusion regarding the role of moral authority in politics. It's a complex dynamic that evokes both praise and criticism from different perspectives.

This evolution reflects a broader trend where political ambitions can overshadow foundational principles of leadership that are rooted in the Black church. While striving for social justice and equality is vital, the emphasis on a political agenda can detract from original spiritual missions, leading some community members to feel that the focus has shifted from uplifting souls to accumulating political power.

Moreover, the styles of leadership embodied by celebrities and athletes further complicate the discourse on effective leadership in the Black community. Today, many look to figures like Lebron James or Colin Kaepernick, who leverage their platforms for social issues. While their influence can indeed inspire change, this celebrity-driven approach often prioritizes charisma and media presence over the essential characteristics of assertiveness and conviction that resonate deeply within traditional leadership models. In many cases, the actions of these figures are based on their celebrity status rather than established roots within the community, leading to a dilution of the substantive, relational leadership found in more traditional settings.

Leadership styles characterized by excessive vulnerability or emotional expression can also lead to perceptions of indecisiveness or lack of direction. While emotional intelligence is undoubtedly critical in effective leadership, striking a balance is essential. Overemphasizing vulnerability can be misinterpreted as weakness, leading some community members to seek leaders who display confidence and the ability to make tough decisions in challenging times. The imperative for assertiveness and conviction in leadership is particularly pressing in a society faced with systemic inequalities and ongoing struggles for justice.

While the landscape of leadership in the Black community is evolving, the essential qualities of assertiveness, responsibility, and decisiveness remain crucial. Leaders who can balance emotional intelligence with strong, unwavering conviction will continue to inspire and mobilize communities. Thus, while engaging with political platforms and celebrity influence has its place, returning to the core tenets of traditional leadership rooted in the church may better serve the community's long-term aspirations and moral direction.

Reclaiming Cultural Narratives

Cultural narratives significantly influence societal perceptions and attitudes toward various identities, including race and gender. Black masculinity has often been framed through a lens of stereotypes—

characterized by violence, criminality, and emotional deficiency. However, these narrow portrayals fail to encompass the rich and diverse experiences of Black men, particularly in the context of leadership. Reclaiming and reshaping the narratives around Black masculinity is crucial for highlighting the strength, resilience, and assertive leadership qualities that many Black men embody.

The Impact of Cultural Narratives

Cultural narratives serve as frameworks through which individuals interpret their experiences and the world around them. In the case of Black masculinity, dominant narratives have often been shaped by media representations, historical contexts, and systemic inequalities. The "thug" stereotype, for instance, undermines recognition of the complexities and strengths found in Black masculinity, perpetuating biases that affect everything from personal interactions to legal judgments.

Stereotypes of Black masculinity can generate self-fulfilling prophecies, influencing how Black men see themselves and how society perceives their actions. For young Black men, these narratives can limit opportunities, perpetuate discrimination, and hinder personal development. When positive examples of assertive leadership and constructive masculinity are overshadowed, the potential for change and growth is diminished.

Celebrating Strong, Assertive Male Leadership

Reclaiming cultural narratives about Black masculinity involves amplifying examples of strong, assertive male leadership. Figures such as Martin Luther King Jr., Malcolm X, and contemporary scholars like Khalil Gibran Muhammad serve as counter-narratives to stereotypical views. Their leadership styles exemplify determination, resilience, and a commitment to community upliftment. Khalil Gibran Muhammad, in his role as a historian and educator, not only engages with the complexities of Black history but also emphasizes the importance of narrative in shaping social justice, thereby challenging notions that equate masculinity with aggression and dominance. Instead, he presents a vision of leadership rooted in integrity, advocacy, and collaborative efforts.

Promoting alternative narratives can also involve recognizing the everyday leadership of Black men in various contexts—families, communities, and workplaces. For instance, the roles of Black fathers, educators, and mentors contribute to the reclamation of a narrative that celebrates nurturing, wisdom, and strength. These men demonstrate that assertiveness need not be synonymous with aggression but can also encompass advocacy, support, and empowerment of others.

Pushing Back Against Diminishing Stereotypes

To effectively push back against stereotypes that diminish Black masculinity, it is essential to engage in various forms of activism and education. This can take the form of community programs, mentorship initiatives, and media representation that focus on the positive contributions of Black men. Collaborations with filmmakers, authors, and artists can help create and disseminate narratives that counter stereotypes, providing a platform for diverse representations of Black masculinity.

Educational institutions also play a fundamental role in reshaping narratives. Curriculums that highlight the contributions of Black men in history, arts, sciences, and social justice can foster a more nuanced understanding of their identities and roles in society. Conversations surrounding equity, feminism, and intersectionality can further elucidate how Black masculinity intersects with other identities, enriching the overall narrative landscape.

Reclaiming cultural narratives around Black masculinity is not merely an ideological exercise; it is a necessary step towards dismantling stereotypes that have persisted for generations. By celebrating strong, assertive leadership while nurturing a more accurate representation of Black men in society, we contribute to a cultural shift that recognizes their complexities and contributions. This reclamation is vital for empowering future generations of Black men, allowing them to see themselves as capable leaders and changemakers, unconfined by limiting stereotypes. Through intentional efforts in storytelling, education, and community activism, we can foster an environment where Black masculinity is celebrated and acknowledged in its full richness and diversity.

Building Community Through Leadership
The Role of Black Men

In the context of Black communities, the absence of positive male role models and leaders can have a profound impact on the development and well-being of younger generations. The question "Where is your daddy?" is often a poignant reminder of the lack of engaged fathers and male figures in the lives of many Black children. This void can lead to a sense of disconnection and a lack of direction, making it challenging for young people to navigate life's challenges.

However, there are many examples of Black men who are actively engaged in leadership positions within their communities, and their impact is profound. These leaders not only provide guidance and mentorship but also serve as positive role models, demonstrating the importance of community engagement and civic responsibility.

This reality was vividly reflected one day in a vibrant community center, where two teenagers, Zephyr and Quinlan, were deep in conversation about their hopes and aspirations. As they leaned against the wall, a hint of frustration colored Zephyr's voice. "You know what really gets to me? Sometimes I wonder... where is your daddy?"

Quinlan paused, his brow furrowing. "Are you asking me where mine is?" he asked, a hint of vulnerability surfacing in his tone. "Because I've been wondering that about myself, too. That question feels heavy, like it's a part of this bigger issue we face."

Zephyr nodded thoughtfully, his expression serious. "Yeah, I was thinking about it in general, but honestly, it feels like a personal question for a lot of us. My dad's been out of the picture for as long as I can remember. It's like trying to solve a puzzle without all the pieces. It's not just about fathers; for a lot of Black men in our community, it's about the absence of strong male figures that shapes our lives. Without that guidance, it's like navigating through a maze blindfolded."

Quinlan looked out the window, watching the younger kids outside playing and laughing. "You know, I think about them a lot. They don't just need role models; they need men who are actively involved in their lives, men who can lead by example. Our community needs to see Black men in positions of leadership—men who aren't afraid to engage and lift others up."

Zephyr agreed, his voice filled with conviction. "Absolutely. It's crucial for our generation to have engaged leaders who can provide structure and a sense of belonging. Leadership isn't just about authority; it's about community engagement. When men step up, it shows younger kids that they matter—that their futures can be different."

Feeling inspired, Quinlan added, "Engaged male leaders can shift the narrative. They can challenge the statistics that show the absence of fathers and instead create legacies of involvement. Imagine if more men became mentors, coaches, or even community advocates. They would create pathways for the younger generation and offer perspectives that we often miss."

As they spoke, the energy in the room changed, and ideas began to form. "What if we started something ourselves?" Zephyr suggested. "A mentorship program or a leadership workshop where older men in our family and community come together to teach those skills. We could invite fathers, uncles, and even older brothers to share their experiences."

Quinlan's eyes lit up with excitement. "Yes! And it can be more than just talking about it. We can engage them in community service, create volunteer opportunities, and show them the impact of their involvement. For every 'Where is your daddy?' there should be a response that highlights the power of community."

In that moment, Zephyr and Quinlan made a pact. They'd begin organizing community meetings that highlighted the significance of Black men in leadership roles and how their engagement could positively influence future generations. They realized that confronting the absence of father figures wasn't just a personal concern; it was about reshaping their community narrative and standing up for the children who looked to them for guidance.

Through their initiative, they envisioned a vibrant community filled with connected families and engaged leaders. Ultimately, the answer to the question that had once weighed heavily on them—"Where is your daddy?"—would transform from an absence into a legacy of presence. By mobilizing their community and providing avenues for male engagement, they could help rewrite the story of fatherhood and leadership, ensuring that every child felt supported, cherished, and empowered.

Addressing the Consequences of Weak Leadership

The lack of strong male leadership, particularly within Black communities, casts a long shadow across various social dimensions affecting individuals and families. This deficiency does not merely operate on an individual level; instead, it reverberates throughout entire communities, impacting social structures, community cohesion, and the aspirations of young Black men. Understanding these broader implications is essential for identifying paths toward restoration and empowerment.

Social Structures and The Foundations of Community

At the core of any community lies its social structures—networks of relationships that facilitate cooperation and support among individuals. Strong male leadership is integral to bolstering these structures. When robust figures are absent, the community often feels a sense of disorientation. The lack of engaged fathers, mentors, and community leaders can lead to a breakdown of traditional family units and mentorship models that have historically provided guidance and support.

Without positive male role models, young Black men may grow up without clear paths to follow, lacking the mentorship that can direct them toward academic success, effective communication, and emotional intelligence. This absence can lead to an increase in negative influences, as young men may seek validation and guidance from peers or external sources that do not promote constructive behavior.

Moreover, weak leadership can also contribute to an increase in crime and violence, as communities without strong guidance may struggle to maintain social norms and boundaries. When leadership fails to instruct, inspire, or protect, it leaves a vacuum that can be filled by aggression or anti-social behavior, thus leading to a cycle of despair that is difficult to overcome.

Community Cohesion as the Fabric of Unity

Community cohesion is another casualty of weak male leadership. A community thrives on the bonds shared among its members, yet these bonds can fray in the absence of strong guiding figures. Leadership fosters trust, builds relationships, and offers a sense of belonging. When men in a community step up and demonstrate responsibility, commitment, and integrity, they foster an environment where everyone feels valued, creating a collective identity that strengthens community ties.

Conversely, when the narrative is one of absence and disengagement, it becomes challenging to build trust among community members. Distrust may emerge as a diagnostic symptom of perceived neglect, leading to a culture of isolation instead of unity. This becomes especially troubling when young people grow up in environments characterized by fragmentation, which can stifle communication, collaboration, and support networks.

With limited positive interactions with male figures in their lives, young Black men may internalize feelings of inadequacy and isolation, which can perpetuate cycles of disappointment and disenchantment. The absence of strong role models contributes not just to individual struggles but feeds into larger societal issues, leading to mistrust and disillusionment that drive wedges between groups, further complicating community cohesion.

Future Outlook and Aspirations and Self-Image

The implications of weak leadership profoundly affect the future aspirations of young Black men. Leadership plays a crucial role in shaping self-image, goals, and aspirations. When strong male figures are prevalent, they act as living testimonies to what is possible—illustrating that success is attainable through hard work, resilience, and integrity.

Without such examples, young men may struggle to envision their futures meaningfully. They may internalize messages of inferiority, believing that societal barriers are insurmountable and that their dreams are unattainable. This lack of hope can lead to lower academic performance, diminished ambition, and trickle-down effects on mental health and wellness.

Young Black men often wrestle with societal expectations and stereotypes. The absence of positive male leadership only serves to reinforce negative narratives, manifesting a sense of hopelessness that can lead to an identity crisis. If they don't see representation in leadership roles—whether in their schools, neighborhoods, or the broader society—they may not see themselves as capable of stepping into those roles in the future. This results in limited aspirations and inhibits their ability to dream big.

Breaking the Cycle through the Importance of Engagement and Solutions

Recognizing these challenges opens the door for potential solutions aimed at mitigating the damage that weak leadership inflicts on communities. Initiatives that promote mentorship, community engagement, and civic responsibility can catalyze positive change.

One promising approach is to foster male mentorship programs that connect younger individuals with older male figures in the community. These relationships can provide guidance, build self-esteem, and enhance life skills like communication and conflict resolution. When the younger generation can engage with positive role models, they are more likely to internalize those lessons, helping them chart a path toward success.

Moreover, community events, workshops, and support groups aimed at young Black men can create spaces for discussion, collaboration, and empowerment. By fostering dialogues about the unique challenges they face, these initiatives can pave the way for resilience and collective action. Encouraging community involvement can teach young men about their civic responsibilities while also showing them that they matter and can make a difference.

Furthermore, public policy must recognize the critical role of strong male leadership in shaping community outcomes. Investment in community development, educational programs, and resource allocation that promote family engagement can serve as a pathway to re-establishing healthy social structures.

The consequences of a perceived lack of strong male leadership within

Black communities are multifaceted, impacting social structures, community cohesion, and the aspirations of young Black men. Weak leadership can fracture bonds, foster mistrust, and stifle ambitions, creating a cycle of despair that can be challenging to break.

However, recognizing these issues presents an opportunity for meaningful change. By fostering a culture of mentoring, community engagement, and accountability, it is possible to rebuild the social fabric essential for nurturing capable and resilient future generations. Addressing the consequences of weak leadership is not just about lifting up individuals; it is about empowering a community, instilling hope, and paving the way for a future where every young Black man can confidently proclaim their identity—knowing they are valued, supported, and poised to lead.

Creating Spaces for Healthy Masculinity

In contemporary society, the concept of masculinity is evolving, especially for young Black men who often navigate complex cultural landscapes. Traditional masculine values—such as strength, resilience, and leadership—can be instilled in ways that promote mental well-being, accountability, and personal development. By creating supportive environments, we can facilitate positive expressions of masculinity. This section presents initiatives and programs aimed at achieving these objectives, highlighting the importance of creating spaces where young Black men can explore and embrace their identities.

Understanding the Context

To frame the discussion, it is essential to understand the unique challenges faced by young Black men. Research indicates that they are often subjected to societal stereotypes that can lead to negative mental health outcomes. According to the American Psychological Association (2016), young Black men are often influenced by the intersectionality of race and gender, which can manifest in experiences of racial discrimination and pressures to conform to narrow definitions of masculinity.

Additionally, a report from the William T. Grant Foundation (2014) highlighted the need for increased support for young Black men. Research indicates that programs focusing on mentorship and personal development can significantly impact their social skills, self-esteem, and emotional intelligence.

The Need for Safe Spaces

Creating safe spaces is crucial for fostering healthy masculinity. These spaces encourage open dialogue, promote accountability, and celebrate diverse expressions of identity. As an individual, my early experiences in community groups designed for young men helped me understand the significance of such environments. The supportive nature of these spaces allowed me to confront fears, embrace vulnerability, and learn from peers who shared similar goals.

Proposed Initiatives and Programs

1. Mentorship Programs

Establishing mentorship programs that connect young Black men with positive role models in their communities can have transformative effects. Studies show that mentorship leads to improved academic performance and emotional health (Rhodes, 2002). Local organizations can facilitate matches based on shared interests, allowing mentors to guide youth through personal and professional challenges.

For example, a successful (though anonymized) mentorship program I was part of involved experienced professionals who shared insights about becoming accountable individuals in society. They encouraged discussions around aspirations, setbacks, and the importance of maintaining integrity. This not only built confidence but fostered a sense of belonging among participants.

2. Workshops for Personal Development

Implementing workshops that focus on emotional intelligence, communication skills, and conflict resolution can help young Black men navigate their personal and professional lives. Research has shown that these skills are vital for long-term success (Goleman, 1995). Workshops can include activities such as role-playing, group discussions, and exercises that build confidence in expressing emotions.

I recall attending a workshop where facilitators created scenarios that allowed us to practice having difficult conversations with peers. This experience illuminated the significance of vulnerability and reinforced that expressing emotions is a strength, not a weakness.

3. Sports and Physical Activities

Engaging in sports can be an effective tool for promoting healthy masculinity. Traditional sports settings can teach teamwork, discipline, and leadership while simultaneously challenging negative stereotypes. According to research published in the Journal of Sport & Exercise Psychology, physical activities can improve mental health and foster community (Weiss & Chaumeton, 1992).

4. Cultural Retreats and Camps

Organizing cultural retreats that focus on the history, traditions, and achievements of Black men can instill pride and a sense of purpose. These retreats can help young men connect with their ancestry and understand how traditional masculine values have evolved.

5. Utilizing Technology for Community Building

In an age where technology plays a pivotal role in communication, leveraging social media and online platforms can create virtual spaces for dialogue. Establishing online forums where young Black men can discuss issues affecting them—free from judgment—can bridge gaps when physical interactions are limited.

Creating a private online platform where participants could anonymously share experiences and seek advice about various topics, from mental health to personal goals, proved to be invaluable. The support and understanding found in this digital community helped many individuals feel less isolated in their struggles.

Accountability and Personal Development

Accountability is fundamental when creating spaces for healthy masculinity. Each initiative must instill a sense of responsibility for one's actions and the well-being of others. Workshops that emphasize collaborative responsibility can be effective. Group accountability strategies help participants understand the impact of their words and actions on their peers, fostering a sense of community.

For instance, one project I was involved in required participants to set collective goals and hold each other accountable for achieving them. The emphasis on teamwork emphasized that each person's success was interconnected, further reinforcing a sense of solidarity among us.

Evaluation and Continued Growth

To ensure that these initiatives yield positive results, it's essential to implement evaluation mechanisms. Surveys, interviews, and focus groups can assess the impact of programs on participants' self-esteem, emotional awareness, and overall well-being. Gathering feedback allows for continuous improvement and demonstrates a commitment to meeting the needs of young Black men.

A project I facilitated utilized feedback forms after each workshop, allowing participants to reflect on their experiences. The insights gained led to refinements in the program, including more focus on specific mental health topics that participants expressed interest in.

Creating spaces for healthy masculinity is more than just a noble idea; it is a necessary endeavor for fostering emotional well-being, accountability, and personal development among young Black men. By implementing mentorship programs, workshops for personal development, sports activities, cultural retreats, and leveraging technology, we can create supportive environments where young men embrace their identities positively.

Through shared experiences, accountability, and intentional growth, we can empower young Black men to explore their masculinity in ways that uphold traditional values while also embracing the complexity of their identities. Working collaboratively towards this goal can lead to profound societal change, breaking the cycle of negative stereotypes and fostering a generation of empathetic, responsible leaders.

The path to healthy masculinity is not easy, but it is a journey worth embarking upon for the future of our communities and the well-being of young Black men. The stories shared and lessons learned in these environments will have lasting impacts, empowering individuals to thrive as they navigate their unique identities in a complex world.

CHAPTER 6
PATHWAYS TO
HEALING AND GROWTH

In the rich tapestry of Black life, healing and growth are pivotal concepts that resonate deeply within our communities. These processes have always played a central role in our culture, shaped by historical struggles, triumphs, and the ongoing search for identity and purpose. As we navigate the complexities of modern society, it becomes imperative to explore pathways that promote emotional, mental, and spiritual well-being. In this chapter, we will delve into various means of achieving healing and growth, recognizing the importance of community, mentorship, tradition, and spirituality. Central to our discussion is the understanding that Yahweh—known as God in many traditions—serves as a guiding force and a source of strength, manifesting in fresh and innovative approaches to foster resilience.

Understanding Trauma and Healing

The history of Black people is marked by trauma, from the horrific realities of slavery and segregation to contemporary experiences of systemic racism and violence. Understanding this history is essential in recognizing the psychological impacts it has on individuals and communities. This legacy can manifest in various forms, including anxiety, depression, and a pervasive sense of disconnection. Healing is not merely an individual pursuit but a collective journey that calls for the support and participation of the entire community.

Acknowledging and confronting trauma is the first step toward healing. The process involves creating safe spaces where members of the community can freely express their feelings, share their stories, and validate each other's experiences. For many, this process can be facilitated through storytelling—a powerful tool that has always been central to Black culture. Storytelling not only offers a means of processing grief and trauma but also allows individuals to reclaim their narratives, allowing them to find strength in their struggles.

Spirituality and Connection to Yahweh

For many members of the Black church, faith and spirituality are central to their lives. The teachings of Yahweh, as articulated through the rich traditions and practices of the church, provide deep insights into the healing process. These teachings emphasize love, forgiveness, and redemption, nurturing a sense of hope that can catalyze profound transformation within individuals and the community as a whole. The Black church serves not only as a place of worship but also as a source of strength, resilience, and support in the journey toward healing and growth.

Engaging with spiritual texts, prayer, and communal worship can provide comfort and reassurance, guiding individuals toward growth. Additionally, the concept of community—often emphasized in spiritual teachings—invites individuals to support one another, recognizing that healing occurs within the context of relationships. Creating spaces for prayer, reflection, and discussion about faith can deepen one's understanding of Yahweh's role in personal journeys of healing and growth.

Creative Expression as a Healing Mechanism

Artistic expression has been a cornerstone of Black culture, serving as a means of communicating experiences, emotions, and aspirations. Music, dance, visual arts, and literature provide avenues for exploration and release. Embracing creative practices can be an effective way to facilitate healing, as art has the power to transcend words, connecting deeply with emotions that may be difficult to articulate.

Community-based art programs can be especially impactful, allowing individuals to collaborate and share their stories through creative endeavors. These initiatives foster connection and understanding, providing a backdrop for collective healing and growth. For instance, group workshops focused on songwriting, painting, or storytelling can create a safe environment where individuals can express their experiences, learn from one another, and develop resilience through shared creativity.

Collaborations and Collective Empowerment

Building robust relationships within the community is crucial for fostering healing and growth. Collective empowerment initiatives that encourage collaboration among various community stakeholders—such as local organizations, schools, churches, and businesses—can significantly enhance support systems for young Black individuals. By uniting these diverse entities, we can create comprehensive programs that address a range of needs, from education and mental health to career development and personal well-being.

These collaborative efforts can take the form of community workshops, educational events, and resource fairs that highlight available services, champion diverse voices, and promote shared goals. By bringing together different generations, knowledge can be exchanged, and innovative solutions can emerge, fostering a common purpose among participants.

Additionally, specialized forums can be established to address pressing community issues, generating open discussions around mental health, resilience, and identity. These forums not only provide opportunities for learning and growth but also encourage participants to actively engage in advocacy and social change, deepening their commitment to the community. By fostering a collaborative spirit, we can cultivate environments where healing and growth are prioritized, ultimately leading to a more empowered and cohesive community.

Embracing Local Heritage and Practices

Incorporating local traditions and practices can greatly enhance pathways to healing and personal growth. Many cultures emphasize the importance of community bonds and shared responsibility, demonstrating how interconnectedness enriches individual and collective well-being. Engaging in local rituals, celebrations, and gatherings offers opportunities for individuals to connect with their heritage and foster a deep sense of belonging.

One effective approach is to create community healing circles or events that draw on local customs and shared experiences. These gatherings provide safe spaces for participants to share their stories, seek wisdom from community elders, and engage in traditional activities such as storytelling, music, or movement. By emphasizing local heritage, these initiatives help reinforce identities and promote a sense of community healing.

Additionally, exploring alternative wellness practices—such as nature-based therapy, traditional arts and crafts, or mindfulness practices rooted in local customs—can introduce innovative strategies for well-being. These often-overlooked methods can complement conventional healthcare, offering holistic solutions that honor local traditions while addressing mental, emotional, and physical health. By revitalizing and integrating local practices, we create pathways to healing that resonate deeply with individuals and communities, empowering them to thrive in a supportive environment.

Education and Empowerment

Launching educational initiatives that empower young Black individuals with knowledge about mental health, self-care, and resources is crucial. Culturally relevant workshops, seminars, and discussions can equip individuals with tools to navigate the complexities of their experiences. These programs can break the stigma surrounding mental health, encouraging open conversations about emotional well-being and personal growth.

Engaging with local schools and community organizations allows for the development of programs that address specific issues faced by young people. Involving parents, educators, and community leaders can create a holistic approach to education, focusing not only on academic success but also on emotional intelligence and resilience.

Pathways to healing and growth require a multifaceted approach. Central to these endeavors is the belief in Yahweh as a guiding force—an embodiment of love, hope, and resilience that transcends life's challenges. By weaving together spiritual principles and innovative approaches, communities can foster environments where individuals feel empowered to heal and grow together.

As we journey along these pathways, it is vital to remember that the struggle for healing is both personal and collective. Each individual's journey contributes to the overall strength and resilience of the community. By working together, supporting one another, and celebrating the unique experiences that shape our identities, we can pave the way toward a brighter, healthier future for generations to come. The journey may be long, but the spirit of our ancestors and the teachings of Yahweh guide us in our purposeful pursuit of healing and growth.

Strategies for Young Black Men to Overcome the Impacts of Father Absence

Overcoming the challenges of fatherlessness is a crucial journey for many young Black men, who often face a unique set of obstacles rooted in the absence of a father figure. This absence can influence various facets of life, from emotional well-being to social interactions and aspirations. However, rather than framing father absence purely as a setback, it is vital to recognize the resilience and strength that can emerge from this experience. By exploring effective strategies for navigation and personal growth, young men can transform their narratives. Instead of feeling defined by their circumstances, they have the opportunity to cultivate empowerment and forge fulfilling paths in their lives.

Understanding the Impact of Father Absence

Father absence often correlates with a range of negative outcomes for young men, including lower academic achievement, increased likelihood of engaging in risky behaviors, and challenges with self-esteem and social relationships. However, it is crucial to recognize that these outcomes are not universal; they are influenced by multiple factors, including social support, community resources, and personal resilience. Understanding the emotional and psychological impact of father absence is the first step in discussing strategies for overcoming these challenges.

Young Black men may experience feelings of abandonment, confusion, or anger stemming from the absence of a father figure. These feelings can manifest in various ways, including difficulties in establishing trust with others, struggles with self-identification, and challenges in navigating societal expectations. It is essential to acknowledge these emotions and understand that it is normal to feel the weight of such experiences. By normalizing these feelings, young men can foster self-compassion and recognize the importance of addressing their emotional needs.

Building Supportive Networks

One of the most powerful strategies for overcoming the impacts of father absence is building a strong support network. Positive relationships play a crucial role in helping individuals navigate life's challenges. For young Black men, this may involve seeking mentors, connecting with role models, or developing friendships based on mutual understanding and support.

In addition to mentorship, peer support can serve as a vital resource for young Black men navigating the challenges of father absence. Connecting with peers who share similar experiences fosters camaraderie and mutual understanding. These relationships can create a safe space where young men can openly discuss their feelings, share personal stories, and exchange coping strategies.

Participating in supportive groups or community forums can enhance this experience. For instance, youth organizations, clubs, or online platforms designed for young Black men can provide avenues for forming friendships based on shared backgrounds and struggles. These connections not only offer emotional support but can also lead to collaborative learning and empowerment, as young men encourage one another to pursue their goals and face challenges together.

Additionally, engaging in activities like group sports, art, or volunteering can help build social bonds and a sense of community. Such involvement provides opportunities for cooperation and teamwork, enriching their lives while combating feelings of isolation. By leaning on each other, young men can create a network that bolsters resilience and fosters personal growth.

Embracing Positive Male Role Models

While the absence of a father figure can be challenging, the presence of other positive male role models can significantly influence a young man's development. Uncles, grandfathers, older cousins, teachers, coaches, or community leaders can all play important roles in providing guidance and support. These figures can demonstrate healthy masculinity, teach valuable life skills, and instill confidence in young men.

Connecting with these role models can provide young Black men with different perspectives on life and relationships. Engaging with men who have successfully navigated similar challenges can help foster a sense of hope and possibility. Additionally, these role models can serve as examples of resilience, showing that one's circumstances do not determine their future.

Pursuing Academic and Career Goals

Investing in education and career development can also serve as a powerful strategy for young Black men dealing with father absence. Pursuing academic excellence and establishing a career can help individuals build confidence and a sense of achievement, counterbalancing feelings of inadequacy that may arise from father absence.

Setting realistic academic goals and actively seeking educational opportunities can be empowering. Engaging in extracurricular activities, joining clubs, or participating in community service can provide young men with a sense of purpose and belonging. Positive academic environments can also lead to meaningful connections with mentors and peers who share similar aspirations.

Career exploration and skill-building activities should also be encouraged. Whether through internships, apprenticeships, workshops, or vocational programs, these opportunities can help young men develop marketable skills and gain real-world experiences. By envisioning a successful future for themselves, young men can cultivate resilience and motivation despite past challenges.

Strengthening Resilience and Coping Strategies

Resilience is a crucial skill for overcoming adversity, and young Black men can actively work to strengthen their resilience. Resilience allows individuals to bounce back from setbacks and adapt to change, fostering a sense of empowerment in the face of challenges.

Developing coping strategies is an integral part of building resilience. This can involve identifying healthy ways to manage stress, such as engaging in physical activities, pursuing hobbies, or utilizing creative outlets like art and music. Finding constructive ways to express emotions and energy can help alleviate some of the burdens that result from the feelings associated with father absence.

Additionally, fostering a growth mindset—the belief that abilities and intelligence can be developed through hard work and dedication—can enhance resilience. Young men who believe they can overcome challenges and improve their circumstances are more likely to persist in the face of adversity. By recognizing failures as opportunities for growth, individuals can cultivate a more positive outlook on life.

Celebrating Achievements and Progress

Finally, celebrating achievements—both big and small—can help young Black men recognize their strengths and foster a sense of self-worth. Acknowledging personal growth, milestones in education, or successful relationships reinforces the idea that they have the power to shape their narratives.

Creating rituals or practices around celebrating achievements can foster a positive mindset. This could involve sharing successes with friends and family, maintaining a gratitude journal to acknowledge progress, or setting new goals upon accomplishing previous ones.

Celebrating achievements builds confidence and reinforces the idea that despite challenges, personal growth and happiness are attainable.

While father absence presents unique challenges for young Black men, there are a multitude of strategies available to help them navigate this experience successfully.

Ultimately, it is essential to recognize that young Black men hold inherent strengths and capabilities. By focusing on growth, connection, and building a supportive community, they can turn the challenges associated with father absence into opportunities for resilience and personal empowerment. Their journeys may be complex, but with the right tools and support, they can and will thrive.

The Journey of Resilience - A Story of Hope and Healing

Having explored the significance of emotional health and resilience, I reflected on the many avenues available for individuals seeking to navigate their challenges. Effective coping skills and emotional regulation techniques are vital components of this journey. A powerfully illustrative story comes to mind—one that embodies these themes of healing and growth. Allow me to share the story of a young man named Jamal.

Right in the heart of a bustling city, Jamal was like many teenagers filled with dreams and aspirations, yet he carried within him a profound sadness stemming from the absence of his father. His father had left when Jamal was just a toddler, leaving behind questions and feelings he often struggled to articulate. Growing up without a father figure created shadows that sometimes felt suffocating. Jamal grappled with complicated emotions—anger, confusion, and an aching loneliness—that followed him throughout his youth.

Despite the love and resilience of his mother, who worked tirelessly to provide for him and his three younger siblings, Jamal often felt like a burden. Their conversations danced around topics of loss and absence, rarely diving into the emotions that simmered beneath the surface. Instead, they filled the void with laughter and distractions, but inside, Jamal was wrestling with a whirlwind of feelings that made him feel isolated.

After school, he often retreated to a nearby dilapidated park—his sanctuary. It wasn't anything special—just a few benches, a playground with rusted swings, and a broken basketball hoop—but there, he could unleash his pent-up thoughts. The repetitive rhythm of the basketball bouncing on the concrete became a form of meditation, providing moments of clarity amid the shadows of his mind.

One late afternoon in October, with leaves transitioning to golden hues, Jamal arrived at the park feeling particularly heavy. He had recently struggled with his grades, the demands of school, and the emotional turmoil stemming from his father's absence. As he began to shoot hoops, each miss added to his frustration, igniting a surge of anger within him. "Why can't I just get it right?" he yelled, voice echoing off empty benches, only to be met by the crushing weight of sadness that followed.

In the stillness that lingered, he decided to give his body and spirit some peace. He recalled a deep-breathing technique his mother had taught him: "Inhale deeply... hold... exhale slowly." As he followed those steps, he began to feel lighter. Sitting down at the court's edge, it dawned on him that it was okay to feel this way, that acknowledging his emotions was not a sign of weakness but instead a pathway toward resilience.

Drawing out a worn-out journal—a Christmas gift from his mother—he clicked the pen and began writing about his feelings. Each word flowed freely, transforming his pain into narrative. Through writing, he found emotional regulation, stitching together the raw threads of his experiences into something coherent and hopeful.

Jamal set small goals for himself in these pages, aiming for increments of change that would help him manage his emotions. "Tomorrow, I'll talk to someone about this," he wrote, slowly realizing that opening up might be a step toward healing. That day marked a turning point; he made a plan to approach his favorite teacher, Ms. Thompson, who always encouraged her students to express their feelings.

With a mix of butterflies in his stomach, Jamal approached Ms. Thompson after class. "Can we talk?" he asked, his voice steady despite the anxiety flooding his heart. They found a quiet corner away from the busy halls, and there, Jamal allowed his vulnerabilities to emerge. "I don't have a dad," he confessed quietly, feeling a weight lift as he spoke. Ms. Thompson listened intently, validating his experience without judgment. "Everyone feels loss differently. It sounds like you're carrying a lot," she gently acknowledged.

As the days passed, Jamal integrated mindfulness practices into his routine. Before starting homework, he would sit quietly, focusing on his breath. Deep breathing helped him clear his thoughts, allowing him to tackle challenges without being consumed by frustration. Eventually, with Ms. Thompson's encouragement, he scheduled an appointment with the school counselor.

Walking into the counselor's office for the first time was intimidating. Yet, as they began to talk, Jamal found that opening up didn't make him vulnerable; rather, it offered him strength and clarity. The counselor introduced him to creative outlets such as drawing and writing poetry, further encouraging him to explore his emotions in constructive ways.

With newfound skills, Jamal started to notice shifts not only within himself but also in how he connected with his friends. They began to gather after school, engaging in basketball and sharing openly about their struggles. Vulnerability became not a weakness but a profound strength. One chilly afternoon, he mustered the courage to share his own story. As he opened up about his father's absence, he was met with understanding and support from his friends—many of whom resonated with his experience.

Years later, as Jamal stood at the edge of that same park, now vibrant with new memories, he reflected on the substantial growth he had experienced. From a boy weighed down by grief and confusion, he evolved into a young man brimming with resilience. Transcending his own trials, he began leading workshops to empower young boys navigating similar challenges. He encouraged them to share their feelings, celebrate their triumphs, and cultivate supportive communities.

This powerful story of Jamal exemplifies the pathways to healing and growth. It serves as a reminder that while the shadows of absence may linger, resilience can be cultivated through connection, coping, and creativity. Each of us holds the potential to transform our pain into purpose, guiding ourselves and others toward a brighter future. With every deep breath and every shared story, we discover that healing is not only possible—it is achievable through collective strength and support.

CHAPTER 7
HEALING FOR OUR BLACK FATHERS

In the landscape of fatherhood, particularly for Black fathers, the toll of systemic inequities becomes glaringly apparent, especially when examining the impact of incarceration. The phrase "prison trauma" encompasses a myriad of experiences: the emotional scars of separation from family, the pervasive stigmas, and the psychological effects of institutionalization. For many Black fathers, prison is not merely a physical confinement; it is an emotional and mental landscape that alters their understanding of masculinity, responsibility, and connection to their children.

When they return from prison, they often face enormous barriers—not only external ones like employment and housing but also internal challenges rooted in their experiences behind bars. The trauma they endure can manifest in unhealthy coping mechanisms, a rigid understanding of masculinity, and an inability to navigate the complexities of modern fatherhood. They may come home carrying a mindset shaped by survival tactics honed in a place that stripped them of agency and reinforced emotional detachment.

This chapter will delve into the profound need for healing among these fathers. It will explore the themes of trauma, masculinity, and the transformative journey toward reclaiming personal identity and nurturing relationships. By examining the effects of prison on fatherhood, we can better understand the pathways toward healing that are essential for Black fathers as they strive to reconnect with their families and redefine their roles in society.

The Impact of Incarceration on Fatherhood

Incarceration carries profound implications for Black fathers and their families, primarily through the lens of physical separation. This enforced distance influences not only the father-child relationship but also the dynamics with partners, leading to a pervasive cycle of disconnection that can last for generations. Understanding these experiences reveals the emotional challenges faced by these fathers and underscores the need for strategic interventions to foster reconnection and healing.

At the heart of a father's identity is his role within the family. For many, fatherhood embodies a sense of pride, responsibility, and connection. However, when faced with incarceration, these fathers endure the emotional weight of separation, which often leads to feelings of guilt and inadequacy. The physical barriers of prison walls strip them of everyday interactions with their children and partners, leading to a significant absence in both nurturing and guidance. The deep-rooted connection that fathers share with their children is vital for emotional development, and the abrupt disruption of this bond can have dire consequences on their children's well-being.

Children are often left to grapple with the pain of their father's absence, which can manifest in various emotional and behavioral issues. The abrupt separation can lead children to question their worth, feel abandoned, or develop anxiety stemming from uncertainty about their father's future. Preschool and elementary-aged children, in particular, struggle to comprehend the reasons behind their father's absence, which can fuel a sense of alienation. As a result, these children may display anger, depression, or withdrawn behavior, exacerbating their emotional challenges and perpetuating a cycle of trauma.

The effect on partners is equally significant. Many Black fathers find themselves in relationships strained by the challenges of incarceration. Partners often bear the weight of managing the family's finances and emotional health amid the absence of the father, leading to resentment, frustration, and sometimes the dissolution of the relationship. This dynamic can create a sense of instability, amplifying the gap between the father and family. The partner may also have to navigate the stigma associated with incarceration, leaving both parents feeling isolated from their community and support systems. This isolation can hinder effective communication, which is vital for maintaining any semblance of a healthy relationship.

Further complicating this dynamic is the reality that many Black fathers face upon their release from prison. The societal stigma surrounding incarceration can prevent them from reestablishing their roles within the family unit. They return home not only to the emotional baggage of their experiences in prison but also to the reality that their partners and children have adapted to life without them. In many cases, children may have established new routines or relationships that do not include their fathers, posing challenges for reintegration. Even if a father wishes to reinitiate connections, the emotional distance created by time and circumstances can feel insurmountable.

Moreover, the institutional barriers fathers face can further entrench this cycle of disconnection. Many returning fathers struggle to find stable employment, housing, or support services that can facilitate their reintegration. Coupled with a lack of resources, these barriers can lead to frustration and hopelessness, often causing fathers to withdraw from family interactions. The impact becomes cyclical; the more a father feels disconnected or marginalized, the harder it becomes to engage with his family. This withdrawal can lead to a sense of hopelessness, reinforcing the belief that they are unable to fulfill their roles as active, loving fathers.

Breaking this cycle of disconnection necessitates a concerted effort from both the fathers and the systems surrounding them. Establishing support networks for incarcerated fathers can create pathways for connection during incarceration. Programs that facilitate communication, such as video calls or letter writing, can help maintain relationships even when physical presence is not possible. Reentry programs that focus on not just employment but also relationship-building can provide fathers with tools to mend their family ties.

Community organizations can also play a crucial role in fostering understanding among families experiencing incarceration, promoting empathy, and bridging the communication gaps that arise. When families approach these challenges as a unit—acknowledging the pain and the complexities together—opportunities for healing and reconnection emerge.

The experience of separation due to incarceration for Black fathers deeply affects their relationships with their children and partners, creating a cycle of disconnection that can persist long after they are released. The emotional ramifications are far-reaching, impacting the mental health of children and partners alike. To create healthier family dynamics, it is essential to acknowledge and actively address these challenges, ultimately fostering an environment where connection, understanding, and healing can flourish. By prioritizing supportive interventions, we can begin to dismantle the barriers these fathers face and pave the way for stronger, more resilient family ties.

Black Psychological Trauma and the Mental Health Impacts of Incarceration

Incarceration does not merely confine individuals to prison cells; it leaves deep psychological scars that can impact mental health long after release. For many Black fathers, the experience of imprisonment is often compounded by pre-existing societal traumas, systemic racism, and socioeconomic challenges. The mental health effects of incarceration—including conditions like post-traumatic stress disorder, anxiety, and depression—can severely hinder their ability to engage with their families and reintegrate into society.

Post-traumatic stress disorder is one of the most significant mental health issues that incarcerated individuals face. The traumatic experiences inherent in prison life—ranging from physical violence and sexual assault to witnessing death or serious injury—can lead to lasting psychological harm. For Black fathers, these experiences are often exacerbated by the cumulative effects of racial discrimination and violence both before and during incarceration. The trauma can manifest in persistent flashbacks, nightmares, and hypervigilance, making it difficult for fathers to feel safe or secure in their interactions with loved ones. As they struggle with these experiences, their capacity to nurture and connect with their children diminishes, leading to a further cycle of disconnection and emotional estrangement.

Anxiety is another prevalent mental health issue for formerly incarcerated Black fathers. The uncertainties of reentry into society—stemming from the stigma associated with incarceration, lack of employment opportunities, and the pressure to meet family expectations—can fuel overwhelming feelings of worry and dread. This constant state of anxiety can impair a father's ability to fully engage with his children and partner. Instead of focusing on rebuilding relationships and fostering intimacy, he may become preoccupied with fears about the future, exacerbating feelings of inadequacy. Furthermore, anxiety can manifest physically, influencing a father's ability to participate in family activities or to communicate effectively, leading to frustration and potential withdrawal from family life.

Depression can also run rampant among Black fathers who have experienced incarceration. The weight of incarceration often brings feelings of hopelessness, grief, and despair. Many fathers grapple with the emotional burden of missed milestones in their children's lives, leading to deep-seated guilt and sadness. This emotional pain can be profound, potentially resulting in a lack of motivation to reconnect or engage meaningfully with their families. The stigma of being a "prisoner" can further alienate these fathers, adding to their feelings of worthlessness. When depression takes hold, it becomes increasingly difficult for fathers to fulfill their roles, creating additional strain on their relationships and exacerbating feelings of isolation.

The interplay of PTSD, anxiety, and depression creates a complex web that can significantly hinder a father's ability to effectively engage with his family. This triad of mental health challenges complicates interactions, making it difficult for fathers to be present physically, emotionally, and mentally. When a father battles inner turmoil, his capacity to offer support, love, and guidance is compromised, leaving children and partners without the nurturing presence they need.

Addressing mental health among Black fathers' post-incarceration should be a priority, encompassing trauma-informed care tailored to their unique experiences. Accessible mental health services, community support programs, and resources focused on trauma recovery can provide these fathers with the tools they need to process their experiences and reclaim their roles within the family.

Breaking the cycle of psychological trauma requires acknowledgment and intervention at both individual and systemic levels. By fostering a supportive environment that prioritizes mental health, we can begin to heal the wounds caused by incarceration and empower Black fathers to engage actively and meaningfully with their families once again.

Healing Trauma through Pathways to Recovery

The journey to healing trauma, particularly for Black fathers who have experienced incarceration, is both complex and deeply personal. The impact of imprisonment extends far beyond physical confinement, often leaving emotional and psychological scars that interfere with relationships, self-worth, and the ability to engage with loved ones. However, pathways to recovery are available, including therapeutic approaches and spiritual healing through faith in Yahweh and community support from the church.

Therapeutic approaches play a crucial role in addressing the unique challenges faced by fathers navigating the implications of prison trauma. Counseling and individual therapy offer tailored support to help individuals process their experiences, emotions, and the sense of loss often associated with incarceration. Therapists trained in trauma-informed care can create a safe environment for Black fathers to explore the compounded impact of systemic racism, societal stigma, and personal trauma. This approach emphasizes understanding trauma's effects on mental health and promotes coping mechanisms that empower individuals.

Group therapy adds another layer of healing by fostering connection and shared understanding among those with similar experiences. For Black fathers, being in a supportive environment where they can openly discuss their challenges related to incarceration can lighten the emotional burdens they carry. Group settings provide opportunities for vulnerability, accountability, and solidarity, allowing individuals to witness healing in others while pursuing their own. This collective healing process can help break the isolation that incarceration often engenders.

In addition to these therapeutic methods, the concept of forgiveness emerges as a powerful tool for healing. Forgiveness involves releasing the emotional shackles of anger, resentment, and guilt—a critical step for Black fathers seeking to overcome their past. While many struggle with the weight of their past choices and experiences, it is important to understand that releasing oneself from these burdens is a feasible goal. By letting go of the hold that one's past has on them, individuals can foster personal growth and create an opportunity to embrace a new identity that transcends previous mistakes.

Equally important is the journey of forgiving others who have caused pain. Many fathers harbor resentment towards figures from their past, whether it be authority figures, members of their community, or even family. The act of forgiveness does not condone harmful behavior; rather, it serves as a means of restoring personal peace and reclaiming one's narrative. It opens the door to healing relationships, especially with children and partners who may have been affected by the trauma of incarceration.

Rebuilding trust with children and partners is another crucial aspect of recovery for incarcerated fathers. Trust is the bedrock of familial relationships, and reconnecting after a period of absence requires intentionality and openness. Fathers must communicate honestly about their experiences, convey their desire for involvement, and express love and commitment to their families. Being vulnerable, sharing their progress toward healing, and actively engaging in activities that foster connection can establish a foundation for renewed trust.

The role of faith cannot be overlooked in this healing journey. Turning to Yahweh, many find solace, strength, and a sense of purpose that transcends their past. Spirituality can provide a framework for understanding suffering and redemption, helping individuals tap into an inner resilience they may not have known existed. The church can serve as a community support system, offering resources, counseling, and a nurturing environment where healing can flourish. Many churches emphasize forgiveness, reconciliation, and the transformative power of faith, helping individuals cultivate hope, restore relationships, and reclaim their identities as loving fathers.

In summary, healing trauma requires a multifaceted approach that integrates therapeutic methods, the power of forgiveness, and the spiritual support found in faith and community. By addressing these elements, Black fathers can navigate their recovery journey, ultimately fostering healthier relationships with themselves, their families, and their communities. Through this process, they can emerge stronger and more resilient, embracing their roles and rebuilding lives marked by love, trust, and hope.

Empowerment Through Black Fatherhood

Fatherhood is a profound journey that offers immense opportunities for growth, connection, and empowerment. For Black fathers, this role is not just a title but a significant commitment that shapes their identities and influences the lives of their children. Finding purpose in fatherhood is essential, as it allows men to step into their roles as caretakers and mentors, making a conscious choice to be actively involved in their children's lives.

Understanding the importance of purpose in fatherhood means recognizing that being a father is not simply a default role that one falls into due to circumstances. Instead, it is a purposeful, intentional decision that requires effort, dedication, and love. Black fathers, particularly those who may have faced challenges such as incarceration or systemic barriers, must be proactive in defining what fatherhood means to them. This approach transforms fatherhood into an empowering experience in which men embrace their roles wholeheartedly, becoming positive influences in their children's lives.

Finding purpose as a father also involves setting goals that extend beyond daily responsibilities. It requires fathers to reflect on their values and the legacy they wish to impart to their children. This could mean prioritizing education, teaching skills, or instilling strong moral principles. When fathers embody these values, they serve as living examples of resilience and strength, encouraging their children to pursue their dreams and navigate life's challenges with confidence.

For Black fathers striving to re-engage in their children's lives, constructing strong family bonds is paramount. This can be particularly relevant for those seeking to reconnect with their children after periods of absence—whether due to incarceration, work commitments, or personal struggles. Active engagement is key; fathers should prioritize spending quality time with their children while fostering communication, understanding, and emotional availability. Regularly participating in activities, whether it's simple outings or shared hobbies, can help build rapport and trust, creating a solid foundation for a healthy father-child relationship.

Additionally, promoting open dialogue and emotional expression is vital in strengthening these familial bonds. Black fathers often benefit from creating safe spaces where their children feel comfortable sharing thoughts and feelings. By actively listening and validating their children's experiences, fathers help cultivate a deep sense of trust. This nurturing environment enables children to express themselves without fear of judgment, ultimately reinforcing the father's role as a supportive figure.

Moreover, Black fathers can play a crucial role in fostering respect within their families. Modeling respectful behavior towards their partners and children teaches valuable life lessons about healthy relationships and mutual support. By demonstrating respect and understanding, fathers not only build stronger connections with their families but also influence their children's perceptions of relationships and self-worth.

Finally, empowerment through fatherhood also involves supporting the holistic development of children. This means ensuring they have access to necessary resources, advocating for their education, and being involved in their school activities. By actively participating in their children's lives and interests, fathers demonstrate their commitment to their children's success and well-being.

In conclusion, empowering Black fatherhood involves recognizing the profound purpose that comes with being a father and taking intentional steps to embody that role. By actively engaging in their children's lives, fostering trust, and prioritizing open communication, fathers can build strong, loving relationships that contribute to a nurturing family environment. Through these efforts, Black fathers not only empower themselves but also become pivotal figures in the lives of their children, shaping future generations and cultivating a legacy of love, strength, and resilience.

Moving Forward And Building a New Legacy

In a world where the roles of fathers are often underappreciated or fraught with challenges, the vision for healed fatherhood becomes a beacon of hope—not only for fathers themselves but for the next generation. This vision is deeply rooted in emotional health, active parenting, and community support, with a powerful spiritual foundation established through the teachings of Yahweh and Jesus Christ. Envisioning what a healed fatherhood looks like, we can create a legacy that moves beyond adversity and hardship, setting a positive example for children that emphasizes love, support, and resilience.

A Shift in Fatherhood

A healed fatherhood embodies the active engagement of fathers who understand their roles as both caretakers and spiritual leaders. Drawing inspiration from the teachings of Yahweh, who calls for justice, love, and compassion, fathers are encouraged to pursue emotional health as a vital aspect of their identities. Emotional intelligence—the capacity to recognize and understand one's own feelings, as well as those of others—forms the bedrock of effective parenting. By embracing vulnerability, fathers can cultivate genuine relationships with their children, demonstrating that it is both courageous and essential to express emotions.

This generational shift is not one that occurs in isolation; it is a collaborative effort fortified through community support and the teachings of Jesus Christ. In the New Testament, Jesus exemplifies the ultimate model of love and relationship. His interactions with others reflect a profound understanding of the human condition, underscoring the importance of connection and empathy. By following Christ's example, fathers today can strive to create environments of safety and respect within their families.

A healed fatherhood entails a community of fathers committed to breaking cycles of silence and emotional repression. Through the lens of faith, these fathers can unite, sharing their stories and fostering relationships grounded in shared experiences and struggles. This collective strength embodies the spirit of accountability and mentorship, thus facilitating healing not only for themselves but also for the children they guide.

Creating Supportive Environments

The journey towards healed fatherhood cannot be undertaken alone; supportive communities play an integral role in fostering environments that nurture Black fathers and celebrate their successes. Such communities can promote healing by providing resources, mentorship programs, and spaces for sharing experiences that validate and uplift fathers facing various challenges.

Much like the early Christian community described in Acts, supportive environments can bring people together to forge bonds of kinship that nurture families. Acts of kindness, mutual support, and celebration of milestones—inspired by the teachings of Yahweh and exemplified in the life of Christ—can create a culture that values the contributions of Black fathers.

Mentorship programs can provide essential guidance for younger fathers, helping them navigate the complexities of parenthood. Drawing from the collective wisdom and experiences of older men can empower younger fathers to embrace their roles with confidence and purpose. By interweaving the lessons of faith with practical advice, mentors can guide fathers toward unlocking their potential.

Additionally, community organizations can host workshops and training sessions that focus on emotional health, conflict resolution, and effective parenting strategies. By equipping fathers with essential tools and knowledge, one can create a powerful ripple effect that positively impacts families. These workshops can also emphasize the importance of faith, offering fathers resources that encourage them to seek guidance through prayer, scripture, and fellowship.

Moreover, creating spaces that celebrate Black fatherhood is crucial. By organizing events that highlight the achievements of fathers, communities can honor their contributions and dispel negative stereotypes. Such celebrations can range from family festivals to community awards, recognizing fathers who exemplify dedication, love, and resilience. Jesus

Christ taught his followers to rejoice with those who rejoice, creating an environment in which every father feels valued and uplifted.

The Spiritual Dimension of Fatherhood

At the heart of healed fatherhood lies a spiritual dimension rooted in faith. Both Yahweh and Jesus Christ offer profound insights that can guide fathers as they strive to redefine their roles. Yahweh, as the eternal Father, embodies the qualities of love, patience, understanding, and discipline. Fathers are called to emulate these virtues as they guide their children on their own paths.

The biblical narrative reminds us that fatherhood is a divine calling rather than a mere societal obligation. As fathers seek to cultivate their spiritual lives, they can draw inspiration from Yahweh's promises of guidance and support. This often involves fostering a personal relationship with God through prayer, reflection, and seeking spiritual community.

Incorporating Christian teachings into the framework of fatherhood can encourage fathers to be active participants in their children's spiritual growth. Whether through family devotionals, attending church services together, or engaging in discussions about values and ethics, fathers can demonstrate the importance of faith in everyday life. Jesus' teachings about love, forgiveness, and service can become guiding principles that influence how fathers relate to their children and community.

Healing from the challenges faced can also involve seeking forgiveness and extending grace to oneself and others. For many fathers, past mistakes or moments of absence may weigh heavily on their hearts. Embracing the redemptive nature of Christ's love underscores the belief that there is always a path forward, characterized by second chances and new beginnings. Acknowledging shortcomings does not define a father; rather, it provides an opportunity to grow and flourish moving forward.

Leading by Example

A healed fatherhood ultimately leads to a legacy defined by empowerment and love. Children learn by observing their parents, and fathers can leave an indelible mark by modeling behaviors that promote emotional health, respect, and understanding. By practicing active parenting—showing up for school events, engaging in conversations about feelings, and participating in shared activities—fathers can instill values that resonate throughout their children's lives.

Jesus Christ emphasized the importance of leading by example: his life was a testament to service, love, and humility. By embodying these values, fathers guide their children on how to engage with the world around them—fostering empathy, resilience, and responsibility. This legacy becomes a powerful tool for breaking generational cycles of pain and hardship, redirecting families toward healing and prosperity.

As the vision for healed fatherhood unfolds, it is clear that collaboration, accountability, and empowerment are vital. By embracing the spiritual teachings of Yahweh and Jesus Christ, fathers can nurture their own emotional well-being and create environments that uplift their children and communities. This holistic approach to fatherhood not only transforms individual families but also contributes to a broader societal shift in how fatherhood is perceived and practiced.

Moving forward toward a new legacy of empowered Black fatherhood requires a collective commitment to healing and growth. As fathers redefine their roles with purpose, supported by their communities, they pave the way for future generations that value emotional health and active parenting. By intertwining the wisdom and teachings of Yahweh and Jesus Christ into their lives, fathers can build a lasting legacy rich in love, support, and resilience. In doing so, they create a world where their children thrive— an enduring testament to the power of healed fatherhood.

CHAPTER 8
COMMUNITY VIOLENCE AND THE BLACK FAMILY

In a society that often overlooks suffering, the violence endured by communities of color, particularly Black families, stands as an urgent crisis that speaks to broader systemic issues in America. The stark statistics are damning: while violence accounts for just 5% of deaths among White men and boys aged 15-24 in California, that figure skyrockets to 26% among Hispanic men and boys and reaches a staggering nearly 50% among Black men and boys in the same age group. These numbers reflect more than just statistics; they echo the devastating reality that too many families are forced to face, leaving scars on lives and hearts that may never heal.

This chapter aims to illuminate the intricate web of violence that is woven into the fabric of Black family life, dissecting how gun violence impacts not only the individuals directly affected but the families, communities, and future generations. The National Institute of Justice has noted that youths living in inner cities suffer from post-traumatic stress disorder at rates higher than those experienced by soldiers returning from combat zones. Moreover, the CDC reports that at least 82% of all firearm homicides in the world occur in the United States. For Black Americans across all 50 states, the average homicide rate is eight times higher than that of their White counterparts. These alarming statistics are not merely numbers; they represent lost potential, shattered dreams, and the obliteration of familial ties.

Against this backdrop of harrowing data and pain, we enter the world of Shaphat Outreach, an organization dedicated to "Breaking the Cycle of Violence and Empowering a Brighter Future" in San Diego. Founded and led by yours truly, Bishop Cornelius Bowser, Pastor of Charity Apostolic Church, Shaphat Outreach strives to embody the powerful scriptural mandate found in Psalms 82:3-4 to "defend the cause of the weak and fatherless; maintain the rights of the poor and oppressed." In this chapter, we will explore how the absence of Black fathers exacerbates the challenges stemming from community violence, while also examining the proactive measures being taken through programs like the No Shots Fired initiative and the Season of Peace.

In the further discussion, we will delve into the conditions that breed violence, examining the cyclical nature of abuse, trauma, and absence that has defined countless Black families. We will explore how Shaphat Outreach aims to dismantle this cycle. Through the lens of faith, community support, and social responsibility, we will highlight how pivotal the role of the family is in combating violence and instilling a sense of hope among the youth.

The Crisis of Violence

To understand the impact of violence on Black families, we must first confront its scope. Gun violence has become an all-too-familiar specter haunting many communities, threatening lives, dismantling families, and undermining the very fabric of society. For Black men and boys, the threat is distinctly pronounced, illustrated vividly by the stark data. The harsh truth is that they are disproportionately affected, often becoming victims of the very violence that surrounds them.

The effects of this violence do not merely result in physical injury or death; they penetrate the emotional and psychological realms of society. A staggering revelation presented by the National Institute of Justice reveals that youth in inner-city neighborhoods suffer from post-traumatic stress disorder—often at rates exceeding those of combat soldiers. How can a thriving future emerge from a foundation built on trauma, loss, and fear? The responsibility to break this cycle falls not only on individuals but on families and communities as a whole.

The role of the Black father is particularly emblematic within this narrative. The absence of paternal figures has been identified as a key factor in perpetuating cycles of violence and disruption within families. According to various studies, children in homes without fathers are more likely to engage in harmful behaviors and encounter adverse life circumstances. These correlations can create a self-fulfilling prophecy, where the absence of a father figure contributes to increased vulnerability to violence, which in turn exacerbates the absence of parental support in future generations.

In this light, we see how violence acts as both a catalyst and a result of structural inequities facing Black families. The statistics reveal a relentless cycle: absence breeds vulnerability, which, in turn, intensifies violence, thus perpetuating further absence. For many, the tragedy is compounded by the reduced support systems available to families; when fathers are absent, roles often fall to mothers who may also be grappling with their own challenges.

The Role of Shaphat Outreach

As I navigate the challenging landscape of community violence that has long plagued our neighborhoods, I find myself driven by a compelling vision of hope and empowerment. Within this maze of despair stands Shaphat Outreach, a faith-based initiative that I am proud to lead. Our mission is clear: we aim to empower individuals to break the cycle of gun and gang violence and embrace the possibility of positive change.

But our work transcends mere intervention; it is a holistic approach designed to foster a sense of community rooted in resilience, empathy, and collective responsibility. We believe that each individual possesses the potential for transformation, and it is through the power of faith and a united community that we can ignite lasting change.

As I reflect on the urgent need for this initiative, I am continually reminded of the profound impact of violence on Black families—an issue that demands not only our attention but also our active engagement. In my role as a pastor and community leader, I have witnessed firsthand the trauma, fear, and instability that violence instills in families. It is this reality that fuels my commitment to the work we do at Shaphat Outreach.

Together, we strive to redefine what the future can look like for our community, challenging the pervasive narratives that often define us. By providing resources, support, and spiritual guidance, we seek to empower individuals—particularly the youth—to choose pathways that lead away from violence and toward hope and healing. In doing so, we are not just addressing the symptoms of violence; we are taking decisive steps to dismantle the deeper societal issues that give rise to it.

At the heart of Shaphat Outreach lies the No Shots Fired (NSF) program initiative, which employs a multifaceted approach to combating violence. NSF focuses on gun violence prevention, core intervention, and hospital-based violence intervention—aiming not only to reduce the immediate threat posed by violence but also to transform community norms concerning violence. This transformative work is particularly crucial when we consider the overwhelming impact that violence has on family structures.

Through programs like interactive journaling, cognitive behavioral therapy (CBT), Shaphat Outreach emphasizes the importance of goal-setting and establishing life trajectory plans for high-risk youth. This methodology serves as a powerful tool for change, enabling individuals to envision a brighter future while breaking free from the constraints of their environment. The establishment of goals creates a sense of agency among young participants, empowering them to take control of their futures.

One component of the NSF program is the "Season of Peace," which emphasizes proactive engagement with potential gang members and individuals at risk of violence. These non-violent conversations foster relationships that allow community members to articulate their desires for change, while simultaneously providing an opportunity for Shaphat Outreach to identify individuals who may wish to exit gang culture.

In times of peace, the community can rally together to celebrate its members, strengthening the foundations upon which families are built. It is through these collaborative efforts that the cycle of violence can begin to unravel, allowing families to reclaim their narratives and communities to restore a sense of safety.

Through comprehensive programs like the No Shots Fired initiative and community engagement efforts such as our Season of Peace, we actively create opportunities for transformation. Our collective efforts are anchored in a shared belief: that it is possible to break free from the cycles of violence and despair that have cut so deeply into the fabric of our families and communities.

As we embark on this journey together, I invite you to join us in envisioning a brighter future—one where the safety, well-being, and potential of every individual and family are championed. It is through our faith and commitment to each other that we will overcome the challenges that lie ahead, reclaiming our communities and fostering a legacy of resilience and empowerment for generations to come.

The Impact on Black Families

The intersection of violence and family dynamics can be likened to an intricate dance, one that is often marked by fear, loss, and absence. The impact of gun violence stretches far and wide, rippling through families and communities in ways that are deeply felt and often inadequately addressed. Gun violence does not merely affect the immediate victim; its repercussions linger, casting long shadows over relationships, aspirations, and family structures.

The absence of Black fathers exacerbates the challenges faced by families. When fathers are missing, children are left to navigate the world without parental guidance, often becoming susceptible to negative external influences. Studies show that youth from father-absent households are at an increased risk of encountering violence, whether as victims or perpetrators themselves. The emotional toll is equally burdensome: children may struggle with feelings of abandonment, low self-worth, and a lack of direction, further perpetuating cycles of trauma and violence.

In families affected by violence, the emotional landscape is often fraught with fear. Parents grapple with the pervasive worry of their children becoming victims or, conversely, becoming involved in cycles of violence themselves. This constant cycle of apprehension can create an environment of instability, making it harder for both parents and children to focus on goals and aspirations.

The significance of emotional health cannot be overstated, particularly in the context of Black families facing challenges stemming from violence. When parents are overwhelmed by grief or fear, it becomes increasingly difficult for them to provide the emotional support that children require to heal and thrive. As the Black family unit struggles to navigate these adversities, the need for community support becomes evident.

The Role of Faith and Community

Faith plays an essential role in providing hope and resilience amidst the turbulence caused by community violence. Shaphat Outreach's emphasis on integrating faith-based initiatives within its programs serves as a reminder of the importance of spirituality in healing and empowerment. Within the walls of the Charity Apostolic Church, families are offered a sanctuary where they can come to seek solace, share their struggles, and forge connections with individuals who understand their plight.

Through biblical teachings, families are encouraged to view their circumstances through a lens of faith, emphasizing the need for hope and redemption. This mindset fosters resilience—a critical commodity for families grappling with the aftermath of violence. When individuals find comfort in their faith, they are often better equipped to face life's challenges and envision a better future for themselves and their children.

Moreover, the sense of community cultivated through Shaphat Outreach allows families to forge valuable connections with one another. In an environment where they can share their experiences without fear of judgment, parents can find solace in their shared struggles. These communal bonds can act as buffers against the negativity that violence introduces, providing a support structure that reinforces their aspirations for a better life.

The work being done at Shaphat Outreach exemplifies the power of collective action, championing the idea that change begins at the grassroots level. By providing a space for families to unite in their struggle against violence, the initiative cultivates an atmosphere of empowerment. Through community engagement, families can collaborate on solutions to address violence, thereby laying the groundwork for a more harmonious existence.

The Absence of Role Models and Its Impact on Black Boys

"Where are Black boys going to see Black men? When you look on television, you'll be hard-pressed to name five positive Black men outside the news. Unfortunately, many young people don't go to church, so the last place is the streets, and that's the problem. The streets do a very poor job of making Black men. The real issue is that Black boys have a difficult time seeing strong Black male role models. The conspiracy to destroy Black men comes from White male supremacy. White men are not afraid of White or Black women. The threat to European men will not come from women but from Black men. The best way to destroy Black men is to destroy Black boys." — Jawanza Kunjufu.

In a society increasingly characterized by its portrayal of diversity, the representation of strong, positive Black male role models remains alarmingly insufficient. Jawanza Kunjufu poignantly asks, "Where are Black boys going to see Black men?" While media platforms and public narratives continue to evolve, young Black boys often find themselves deprived of readily available, positive male figures who embody strength, integrity, and resilience. This void poses a significant challenge to their development and self-identity, a concern that has deep-rooted implications for the Black family and community at large.

When reflecting upon portrayals in popular culture and the news, it becomes evident that finding five positive depictions of Black men outside of sports or sensationalistic news coverage is a daunting task. This scarcity can have profound implications for young boys who are looking for mirrors that reflect their potential and worth. With many young people detaching from traditional spaces of engagement—such as church—they often find themselves on the streets, where the examples presented can be increasingly harmful rather than uplifting. Kunjufu's assertion that "the streets do a very poor job in making Black men" speaks to the corrosive influences that can permeate environments where positive guidance is lacking.

The broader societal forces contributing to this crisis cannot be overlooked. Kunjufu argues that the conspiracy to destroy Black men originates from systemic structures rooted in White male supremacy, suggesting that the perceived threat from Black men propels a societal narrative that marginalizes their potential. In essence, when Black boys do not see themselves represented positively, they may begin to internalize negative stereotypes and a diminished sense of self-worth. This detrimental cycle creates a continuous loop of disenfranchisement, impacting not only individual lives but also families and communities.

The consequences of these systemic issues extend well beyond representation; they ripple into the family structure itself. Without strong male role models, young Black boys grapple with their understanding of what it means to be a man in today's world. The absence of father figures or mentors can lead to increased vulnerability to negative influences, diminishing their chances of success in education, social relationships, and future endeavors. Many young boys may not know the importance of character, responsibility, and integrity—traits often imparted through positive male guidance and mentorship.

Addressing this critical gap requires a concerted effort from various sectors of society. Communities must come together to create platforms and spaces for positive Black male role modeling, providing mentorship opportunities where Black boys can engage meaningfully with men who can instill values of resilience, perseverance, and identity. Church and community organizations play a pivotal role in fostering these connections, while media must also evolve to showcase narratives that uplift and empower Black males.

The challenges faced by Black boys in seeking positive male role models are multifaceted, rooted in broader societal issues of representation and systemic inequality. As we strive to nurture a new generation of Black men, we must commit ourselves to dismantling the barriers that obscure their potential and prevent them from seeing the strength and possibility that lies within their community. By doing so, we not only foster individual growth but also contribute to reshaping the narrative surrounding Black men, reinforcing the belief that they can be powerful advocates for change and pillars of strength within their families and communities.

Conclusion

This chapter presents an urgent call to action, challenging readers to confront the pervasive violence that affects Black families and communities across America. The statistics provide sobering evidence of the disparities that exist, and the reality is that lives are lost daily due to gun violence that has permeated neighborhoods. At the same time, organizations like Shaphat Outreach illuminate the possibilities for healing and empowerment.

By examining the impact of violence on the family unit, we recognize the intricate interdependencies at play—the cyclical nature of absence, trauma, and fear. However, we also witness the powerful resilience of families who strive to break free from these cycles. Through faith, supportive communities, and targeted intervention efforts, individuals can reclaim their narratives and foster an environment of hope, healing, and transformation.

Ultimately, the fight against community violence is a collective endeavor that requires commitment from individuals, families, and communities alike. As we move forward, let us remain steadfast in our dedication to building a future that emphasizes healing, empowerment, and unity—a future where the Black family can thrive, free from the shackles of violence and instability. It is through this lens of hope that we can envision a brighter tomorrow for ourselves and generations to come.

CHAPTER 9
LIBERATING THE SOUL OF BLACK MANHOOD

The narrative surrounding Black manhood in America and beyond has often been steeped in the language of victimhood, where systemic and institutional racism creates a profound sense of limitation. From gun violence and policing disparities to economic disadvantages and educational inequities, Black men find themselves caught in a cycle that all too often seems inescapable. This narrative can become a powerful cage, stifling potential and clouding identity. However, there is a path to liberation, one that transcends the constraints imposed by society, and it is found in the profound spiritual truth that true liberation comes through Yahweh, revealed to us through Jesus Christ.

This chapter will delve into the importance of faith in fostering resilience, healing, and empowerment among Black men. By exploring the historical context, current realities, and potential pathways to liberation through a relationship with Christ, we can find renewed hope and purpose in the journey toward overcoming victimhood. The journey of liberation is one that weaves together personal empowerment and a deeper spiritual connection, affirming that in Christ, Black men can rise above limitations and embrace an identity rooted in strength and worth.

The Historical Context of Black Manhood

To fully appreciate the current state of Black manhood, one must first acknowledge the historical context that has shaped its narrative. For centuries, the legacy of enslavement, segregation, and systemic racism has created an environment rife with challenges. Black men have often been framed through lenses of inferiority, violence, and despair. These narratives, perpetuated by media, literature, and societal norms, have had a lasting impact on both perception and self-perception.

However, amidst the historical trauma, the promise of liberation is anchored in faith. Understanding the historical context includes recognizing how faith communities have been sources of strength for Black men. The Church has historically played a pivotal role in advocating for justice, promoting resilience, and fostering a sense of community, making it a significant sanctuary where healing and empowerment can take place.

The Dual Burdens of Systemic Oppression and Spiritual Despair

As Black men navigate the landscapes of systemic oppression—policing practices, economic disparity, and educational inequities—they often encounter spiritual despair as well. The weight of societal expectations and entrenched inequalities can lead to feelings of hopelessness and vulnerability, reinforcing the perception of victimhood. Yet, the teachings of Jesus Christ offer an alternative: a call to rise above these burdens and find purpose amid chaos.

The Cost of Victimhood

While acknowledging the impact of systemic oppression is necessary, it is equally important to understand the cost of adopting a victim mentality. Embracing a worldview defined by victimhood can lead to resignation, despair, and a loss of agency. Black men may internalize societal messages implying that they are powerless to change their circumstances, resulting in a self-fulfilling prophecy.

The message of Christ, however, challenges this narrative. Through his life, teachings, and resurrection, Jesus demonstrated that it is possible to transcend suffering and injustice. His message of love, redemption, and resilience invites individuals to reclaim their narratives, empowering them to rise above the limitations imposed by external forces.

The Path to Liberation Through Healing

Liberating the soul of Black manhood begins with a transformative healing process deeply rooted in one's relationship with Yahweh. Embracing this relationship can provide Black men with the strength and clarity needed to overcome the challenges they face. My personal journey is a testament to this profound truth.

I was once embroiled in a life defined by the West Coast Crips in San Diego from 1974 until my turning point on December 5, 1984. My life revolved around drugs, violence, and repeated stints in county jail. I dropped out of high school and became a father, but I knew little about what it meant to be a dad. Unfortunately, I also confronted the harsh realities of racism and police brutality during these formative years.

I vividly remember an incident that encapsulates this struggle. One day, a police officer from the San Diego Police Department stopped me and some friends. He began to harass us without cause, disrespecting the driver of the car, who was my friend. When I pushed back, the officer seized me, yanked me from the car, and handcuffed me before leaving me standing in the street as he searched my friends. It was a dehumanizing experience that reflected a constant reality for many in my community.

Things escalated when the officer's supervisor arrived. I recognized him because I had previously filed complaints against the SDPD for two shocking incidents: I was kidnapped by officers and taken to the train tracks, where they assaulted me because I wasn't speaking to them with enough "respect." In a separate incident, two officers had robbed me of my money. All this trauma unfolded when I was just 17 years old, laying the groundwork for a life enmeshed in anger and victimhood.

When the supervisor asked what was wrong, I aired my grievances about the treatment I was receiving. His response was unexpected; after speaking with the officer, he approached me, uncuffed me, and offered an apology, saying, "This is the way I was told to treat you guys over here," referring to the Black community. This experience both shocked and infuriated me, leaving a lasting impression on my understanding of systemic injustice. However, it was not until several years later, at the age of 22, that I would encounter the true turning point in my life.

On December 5, 1984, my life took a dramatic turn when I was baptized in Jesus Christ's name and filled with His Spirit. From that moment, Yahweh, through Jesus Christ, liberated my soul; however, I soon realized my mind also required transformation. I was born again in my soul and spirit, yet the journey to renew my mind remains ongoing. Every day brings growth and change, allowing me to shed the victim mindset I once held.

I stand today as a testament to the power of faith and redemption. I have transformed from a life marked by violence and despair into a free Black man grounded in purpose and identity. My relationship with Yahweh has been the bedrock of this transformation, offering me the clarity and strength necessary to navigate life's challenges. Healing is a continuous journey, but with each step, I move further away from my past and closer to the divine calling that fuels my spirit.

Acknowledgment and Understanding

The healing journey begins with acknowledgment. Black men must confront and articulate the traumas they have faced—both collectively and individually. This requires a willingness to be vulnerable and honest about their experiences. Within the context of faith, this acknowledgment can be brought before God in prayer, seeking His guidance and understanding.

Yahweh, through Jesus Christ, offers an invitation for healing and restoration. The act of confession, whether privately in prayer or communally in fellowship, allows individuals to lay down their burdens and begin the process of reclamation. This acknowledgment does not shy away from pain but instead invites divine intervention and healing.

Community Connection Through Faith

Building strong community connections within faith-based contexts is fundamental to the healing process. The Church can serve as a place of refuge, providing teachings that emphasize love, reconciliation, and empowerment. Black men can find support through mentorship programs, Bible studies, and men's groups that foster a sense of belonging and purpose.

In this community, the principles of unity and brotherhood resonate strongly. As Black men engage with one another in faith, they can share their experiences, encourage one another, and build resilience. The collective strength found in community reinforces individual growth and uplifts spirits battered by systemic oppression.

Mental Health and Spiritual Well-Being

Prioritizing mental health within a spiritual framework is an essential step toward holistic liberation. The Church can play a pivotal role in destigmatizing mental health conversations, encouraging Black men to seek support while aligning it with their faith. Whether through pastoral counseling, therapy, or support groups, addressing mental health issues is imperative.

In moments of anguish, turning to scripture and prayer can provide solace and grounding. Verses that emphasize God's love, faithfulness, and purpose can rejuvenate the spirit and empower individuals to move beyond despair. As Black men navigate mental wellness, the understanding that they are beloved creations of Yahweh helps reshape their self-image and reinforces their value.

Education and Economic Empowerment Rooted in Faith

Education is a critical pathway to liberation, and when pursued alongside a strong spiritual foundation, it amplifies potential. Black men must be encouraged to leverage educational opportunities that enhance their skills and knowledge. The Church can be a catalyst for this empowerment, offering workshops, scholarships, and connections to resources that pave pathways to success.

Furthermore, the concept of stewardship within a faith context emphasizes using one's talents for greater purposes. Black men can draw inspiration from biblical principles of entrepreneurship, service, and integrity as they seek to build businesses, create jobs, and uplift their communities. By intertwining faith with economic empowerment, they can break free from the constraints of victimhood and build generational wealth.

Redefining Masculinity Through Christ

The redefinition of masculinity is crucial for liberating Black manhood. Traditional notions of masculinity often dictate that men should be stoic, unyielding, and avoid vulnerability. However, the teachings of Jesus Christ subvert these norms by emphasizing the strength found in humility, compassion, and emotional honesty.

Black men must be encouraged to embrace a holistic understanding of masculinity that allows for vulnerability, nurturing relationships, and emotional expression. Jesus embodied these qualities, teaching that true strength comes from love, service, and sacrifice. By embracing this redefined masculinity through Christ, Black men can liberate themselves from restrictive societal norms that may perpetuate cycles of violence and isolation.

Spiritual Growth as Liberation

Spirituality is a vital force in the healing and liberation process. For many Black men, a connection to Yahweh through Jesus Christ serves as a compass for navigating life's challenges. Engaging in spiritual practices—prayer, worship, and community—provides a sense of hope and belonging.

Christians believe that salvation is not just about being freed from sin; it includes being liberated from the chains of societal oppression and personal despair. The truth of the Gospel affirms that everyone is valued, loved, and capable of transformation. This understanding invites Black men to embrace their identity as sons of God, instilling a sense of purpose and empowerment that transcends their circumstances.

Rising Above Limitations Through Faith

Breaking free from victimhood requires a commitment to personal growth and self-empowerment rooted in faith. Black men must be encouraged to rise above the limitations imposed on them by systemic oppression and societal expectations.

Setting Goals and Aspirations Aligned with Purpose

Establishing clear goals and aspirations, especially those aligned with one's faith, provides direction and motivation. Black men should be encouraged to envision their futures in light of God's promises. This vision allows them to set goals that not only focus on personal success but also contribute positively to their communities.

In prayer, they can seek God's guidance in discerning their paths, ensuring that their aspirations reflect not just their desires but also their divine calling. By aligning aspirations with faith, Black men can boldly pursue a life of purpose.

Celebrating Successes through Gratitude

Recognizing and celebrating successes—both big and small—reinforces a positive self-image and gratitude for God's provisions. Black men should take moments to acknowledge their achievements and express gratitude for the journey. In faith-based communities, sharing these successes can inspire others, reminding everyone that triumph is possible despite obstacles.

Building a culture of celebration helps forge supportive relationships, creating a community that uplifts rather than diminishes. Gratitude, deeply rooted in faith, fosters resilience and encourages continued growth.

Advocating for Change as Servant Leaders

Empowerment extends beyond the individual; it encompasses a collective responsibility to advocate for systemic change in communities often burdened by injustice. Black men can rise as servant leaders, using their lived experiences to uplift others and work toward social justice.

Drawing from the teachings of Jesus, who advocated for the marginalized and oppressed, Black men can engage in efforts to dismantle oppressive systems, promote equity in education and employment, and serve their communities with compassion and integrity. Faith calls them to be change-makers and agents of love in a broken world.

Building Resilience Through Faith

Resilience is an essential characteristic for overcoming adversity, and faith serves as a source of strength in this process. Black men must cultivate resilience by developing coping strategies, leaning on their faith during difficult times, and maintaining a growth mindset that mirrors Christ's journey.

Prayer and meditation can be transformative practices that reinforce mental fortitude and spiritual endurance. When faced with challenges, turning to scripture for encouragement and strength helps Black men cultivate resilience bred from their faith.

The journey to liberating the soul of Black manhood is intricate, interwoven with threads of healing, empowerment, and a deep connection to Yahweh through Jesus Christ. While acknowledging the traumas of systemic oppression is essential, it is equally vital to embrace a mindset of possibility and renewal found in faith. Black men possess the resilience, strength, and potential to rise above victimhood, reclaim their narratives, and redefine what it means to embody Black manhood in this era.

True liberation flows from belief in Christ, who invites individuals to transform pain into purpose, to be agents of change, and to find strength in vulnerability. The Church can be a sanctuary for these transformative journeys, fostering community, promoting mental health, and equipping Black men to embrace their identities as beloved sons of God.

The time for liberation is now, rooted in the essence of faith and the promise of hope offered through Yahweh. The journey toward a brighter future begins within, fueled by a commitment to healing, empowerment, and a deepened relationship with Christ. By fostering these principles, Black men can break the cycles of victimhood and embrace a life characterized by grace, strength, and purpose. Expertly intertwined with faith, this journey is one of both personal and communal liberation, ultimately transforming lives and communities for generations to come.

CHAPTER 10
FATHERS AND SONS RISING

As we reach the final chapter of "Where's Your Father," we stand at a pivotal crossroads where past discussions give way to a powerful reflection on the present and a hopeful gaze toward the future. "Fathers and Sons Rising" embodies not just a theme, but a clarion call for Black fathers and sons to nurture their relationships and uplift one another. This chapter seeks to highlight the intrinsic resilience found within these connections, underpinned by the wisdom and guidance of our faith in Yahweh and Jesus Christ.

In today's world, the relationship between fathers and sons is the bedrock upon which lives are built. It is a dynamic characterized by love, mentorship, guidance, and responsibility. Yet, it is often said that fathers shape the identities of their sons, molding them into men who will one day stand tall in their own communities. The biblical narrative reinforces this idea, as seen in the story of David and Solomon, where wisdom, legacy, and faith are passed from father to son, directing future generations.

As we delve deeper into this chapter, we will explore the transformative power of connection—how Black fathers and sons can rise together, overcoming the challenges faced in society, finding strength in their faith, and nurturing a legacy that reflects their divine purpose. Our journey will be enriched by scriptural insights that remind us of our responsibilities, affirm our identities, and inspire growth as we express the love of Christ in our relationships.

The Power of Connection
The Role of Fathers in Identity Formation

In the intricate design of families established by Yahweh, the father-son relationship holds a distinguished and sacred place. This connection is more than mere biology; it is a foundational bond that shapes the trajectory of young lives and influences their identity formation in profound ways. In Proverbs 22:6 (NIV), the wisdom imparted is clear: "Start children off on the way they should go, and even when they are old they will not turn from it." This verse encapsulates the responsibility fathers have in guiding their sons, ensuring they are rooted in solid morals and values long before they encounter the complexities of adulthood.

For Black families, the role of a father can carry additional layers of significance due to the myriad challenges often faced in society—systemic inequalities, cultural stereotypes, and economic pressures. In such an environment, fathers must not only be providers but also spiritual leaders who instill a sense of purpose, resilience, and identity in their sons. This dual role is crucial, as sons look to their fathers not just for survival but for the guidance that helps them navigate their place in a world that can sometimes feel hostile or dismissive.

Fathers cultivate their sons' sense of identity through actions, teachings, and shared experiences. In many ways, a father's presence—or absence—can profoundly influence a young man's understanding of who he is and where he fits into the world. When fathers actively engage in their sons' lives—whether by sharing stories, teaching life skills, or modeling ethical behavior—they provide a blueprint for identity that is deeply rooted in love and respect.

Moreover, the spiritual aspect of fatherhood cannot be overstated. In Biblical teachings, fathers are charged with the duty to nurture their children in faith. This spiritual guidance creates a framework within which sons can build their values and ethical compass. Through prayer, worship, and discussions about life's purpose, fathers help their sons establish a relationship with Yahweh that transcends generations. When fathers embody spiritual integrity and authenticity, they create a safe space for their sons to explore their faith and understand their identity in God's eyes, leading to a more profound sense of self-worth and belonging.

Moreover, in the face of societal adversities, fathers serve as role models displaying resilience, strength, and vulnerability. The lessons instilled through shared resilience against challenges teach sons to embrace their identities with pride and confidence. In teaching sons how to confront adversity with faith and determination, fathers lay a foundation for positive identity formation that prepares their sons to rise against societal pressures.

The role of fathers in the identity formation of their sons is undeniably crucial. Fathers serve as the guiding stars in their children's lives—lighting the path and helping them navigate the intricate journey of self-discovery. As spiritual leaders, mentors, and role models, Black fathers must recognize the profound impact they have in shaping not only their sons' immediate identities but also the legacy that influences future generations. When they take their roles seriously, they not only fulfill a divine calling but also fortify the family structure, ensuring that their sons stand tall in their identity and purpose, equipped to face the realities of an ever-changing world.

Faith as a Foundation

The bond between fathers and sons is one of the most profound relationships one can experience, and this connection can be deeply enriched through the principles of faith. The teachings of Jesus Christ provide a framework for understanding and nurturing this vital relationship, emphasizing themes of unconditional love and forgiveness. These Christian values are not only powerful in spiritual contexts but serve as fundamental building blocks for strong, resilient family ties.

Ephesians 6:4 (NIV) serves as a guiding principle in nurturing father-son relationships: "Fathers, do not exasperate your children; instead, bring them up in the training and instruction of the Lord." This scripture highlights the responsibility fathers have to engage with their sons positively. It emphasizes that approaching parenting from a standpoint of love and respect is vital for healthy communication and mutual understanding. Instead of fostering frustration through unrealistic expectations or harsh criticism, fathers are called to cultivate an environment conducive to growth and emotional well-being.

At the heart of this nurturing process is the concept of unconditional love—love that accepts and supports regardless of circumstances. Jesus modeled this throughout His ministry, as He embraced people from all walks of life, offering forgiveness and hope. Fathers who embody these principles create secure foundations for their sons, allowing them to explore their identities and relationships without fear of rejection. This atmosphere of acceptance cultivates trust, enabling sons to approach their fathers with their challenges and vulnerabilities.

Moreover, forgiveness is another critical aspect that strengthens the father-son bond. All relationships face trials, and misunderstandings can lead to emotional distance. By practicing forgiveness, fathers teach their sons to embrace a spirit of grace, understanding that mistakes are a part of life. This mirrors the teachings of Christ, who said in Matthew 6:14 (NIV), "For if you forgive other people when they sin against you, your heavenly Father will also forgive you." By modeling this principle, fathers can remind their sons of the importance of resolution and empathy in personal relationships.

Fathers can also leverage their faith as a platform for regular engagement with their sons. Incorporating biblical teachings into everyday conversations and family practices can foster deeper connections. Activities such as prayer, scripture study, and church participation create shared experiences that not only strengthen their faith but also enhance their bond. These engagements provide a shared language that transcends generational gaps, allowing fathers and sons to discuss life's complexities in a context rooted in spiritual values.

Furthermore, faith-based discussions can serve as a means of imparting essential life lessons. Real-life applications of scriptural values can help sons understand how to navigate the moral complexities of the world. As fathers share their own journeys of faith, they provide relatable examples of how adherence to Christian principles can guide decision-making and shape character.

The connection between fathers and sons is profoundly enriched when anchored in faith. The teachings of Jesus, emphasizing unconditional love and forgiveness, serve as vital pillars for nurturing strong familial ties. As fathers engage with their sons positively and constructively, they not only foster environments where love and respect flourish but also create lasting legacies rooted in spiritual integrity. The journey of parenting through faith not only benefits the immediate relationship between fathers and sons but reverberates through generations, influencing the family's legacy and instilling core values essential for a fulfilling life rooted in faith.

Overcoming Challenges Together

Systemic inequalities and societal stereotypes create a landscape fraught with obstacles that can seem insurmountable. These challenges manifest in various spheres, including education, employment, and criminal justice, often creating a cycle of disadvantage that is difficult to break. However, when fathers and sons unite, they form a bond that can challenge these societal issues, providing a foundation of strength, resilience, and mutual support.

The relationship between fathers and sons is critical in shaping self-identity and instilling values that promote perseverance. When fathers engage actively in their sons' lives, they can provide a sense of stability and guidance that counters the negative narratives often perpetuated by society. This involvement can take many forms: mentorship, open communication, and encouragement to pursue education and career aspirations without being hindered by stereotypes. The message becomes clear: they are not alone in their struggles; instead, they have a partner willing to stand beside them.

The biblical affirmation found in John 16:33 resonates deeply within this context. Jesus' assurance of overcoming the world speaks to the inherent strength in unity and faith. Fathers can draw inspiration from this promise, conveying that while struggles are indeed a part of life, they don't define one's destiny. Instead, they can be seen as opportunities for growth and resilience. By sharing this perspective, fathers help their sons cultivate a positive mindset, encouraging them to confront challenges rather than retreat in fear or despair.

Moreover, fathers can model how to navigate and resist the stereotypes that society imposes on Black men and boys. It is important for fathers to discuss their experiences and the ways they have overcome adversity throughout their own lives. This sharing of personal narratives serves not only as practical guidance but also as an inspirational testament to the possibility of greatness despite systemic barriers. When sons witness their fathers standing firm against discrimination and inequality, they learn to adopt similar resilience.

In addition, the collective nature of overcoming challenges draws attention to the importance of community. Fathers and sons can engage with others in their community, forming networks that provide additional support. Participating in local organizations, or father-son initiatives can create a sense of belonging and shared purpose. These experiences reinforce the idea that their struggles are not faced in isolation but are shared within a larger context that requires solidarity and strength.

As systemic inequalities continue to challenge Black men and boys, it becomes increasingly crucial to empower young hearts and minds, allowing them to believe in their potential and worth. In this light, the act of overcoming challenges together evolves into a powerful statement of resilience. By nurturing a strong, supportive relationship, fathers equip their sons with the tools to resist and dismantle the stereotypes that seek to diminish them and instill in them a lifelong belief in their ability to rise above adversity.

The journey of overcoming challenges is best navigated in unity. When fathers and sons stand together, they create a powerful synergy, encouraging each other to confront and surmount the complexities of life. Through open dialogue, shared experiences, and the strength of faith, they can build a legacy of resilience that not only transforms their own lives but also inspires future generations. As they tackle the inherent struggles of their existence, they can emerge not only as survivors but as thrivers, crafting a narrative of triumph that reverberates far beyond their immediate circumstances.

Mentorship and Legacy Building

Mentoring is not merely about offering traditional guidance but encompasses actively preparing young individuals to make meaningful contributions to society. For Black fathers who have faced socio-economic struggles, their experiences render them uniquely equipped to serve as invaluable role models for their sons. By sharing lessons on resourcefulness, perseverance, and the transformative power of faith, they actively shape a legacy that can have profound effects on their families and the broader community.

The concept of mentorship extends beyond surface-level advice; it entails a deep commitment to fostering growth and empowerment. Many Black fathers, having navigated systemic barriers and societal prejudices, often hold insights that are not easily gleaned from textbooks or mainstream narratives. Their lived experiences serve as rich teaching moments that can guide their sons through challenges that may arise in life. For instance, a father's narrative about overcoming obstacles, whether related to education, employment, or systemic discrimination, not only nurtures resilience but also instills a belief that adversities can be faced head-on and conquered.

The teachings passed down by fathers often instill values of resourcefulness and creativity. Fathers can impart wisdom regarding financial literacy, entrepreneurial endeavors, and practical life skills, emphasizing the necessity of resourcefulness in overcoming economic hardships. These lessons empower sons to think outside the box and cultivate skills that extend far beyond immediate circumstances. This kind of preparation builds a robust foundation for future success, allowing young men to transition smoothly into adulthood and navigate various aspects of life with confidence.

Furthermore, the role of faith as an anchor during challenging times cannot be understated. Fathers who emphasize the significance of faith cultivate resilience and hope within their sons. By sharing personal stories of faith during trying times, fathers can help their sons understand that while the journey may be fraught with difficulties, belief in a greater purpose can offer solace and strength. This can create a framework for handling life's unpredictability, instilling hope that transcends present circumstances.

The legacy of mentorship established by Black fathers can echo across generations, leading to the strengthening of communities. As embodied in 2 Timothy 2:2 (NIV), the importance of passing down wisdom is underscored: "And the things you have heard me say in the presence of many witnesses entrust to reliable people who will also be qualified to teach others." This biblical passage emphasizes the cyclical nature of mentorship — it is about equipping the next generation not only to learn but also to teach and inspire others. As sons absorb the wisdom from their fathers, they become bearers of that knowledge, ready to impart lessons to their peers, siblings, and eventually their own children.

In this manner, mentorship transcends the individual and fosters a communal spirit. As young men internalize and then pass along the wisdom they have received, they contribute to a legacy that raises the collective consciousness, resilience, and strength of their community. They begin to advocate for one another, uplift their peers, and create networks of support that encourage everyone to thrive.

Mentorship and legacy building are vital components of Black fatherhood that extend far beyond familial relationships. By embracing their roles as mentors, fathers not only prepare their sons for the challenges of life but also craft legacies that will inspire future generations. Through the shared journey of mentorship, they foster resilience, resourcefulness, and community while nourishing an enduring legacy that echoes through time. In this way, mentorship becomes a transformative force that shapes not just individuals but the fabric of society itself.

The significance of communication in the father-son relationship cannot be overstated. Open lines of communication are foundational for fostering trust, understanding, and a lasting emotional connection. Fathers who prioritize honest and open dialogue create an environment where their sons feel safe to express their feelings, fears, and aspirations. In this nurturing space, communication becomes a tool that not only strengthens the bond between fathers and sons but also cultivates emotional intelligence and resilience.

Creating a Safe Space for Communication

Creating a safe space for communication begins with fathers actively listening to their sons. It requires setting aside distractions and being fully present during conversations. This attentiveness signals to sons that their thoughts and emotions are valued and respected. When fathers demonstrate that they are genuinely interested in what their sons have to say, it encourages boys to open up about their experiences and challenges. This two-way dialogue fosters trust, allowing sons to share their innermost concerns without fear of judgment or reproach.

Biblical wisdom reinforces the importance of this endeavor. Proverbs 20:5 (NIV) states, "The purposes of a person's heart are deep waters, but one who has insight draws them out." This scripture highlights the profound realities that may lie beneath the surface of a son's thoughts and feelings. It underscores the critical role fathers play in unraveling these complexities through insightful questioning and active listening. Fathers who seek to understand the "deep waters" of their sons' hearts not only gain valuable insight into their emotional worlds but also equip their children to navigate those depths on their own.

Communication also serves as a powerful mechanism for instilling emotional intelligence. When fathers engage in open conversations about feelings—whether it's joy, sadness, frustration, or fear—they model emotional literacy for their sons. By discussing emotions, fathers help their sons identify and articulate their feelings, which is essential for emotional awareness and regulation. This practice not only enhances the father-son connection but also prepares sons to empathize with others, fostering healthier relationships in their personal and social lives.

Moreover, open communication helps dispel generational disconnects and allows for the sharing of wisdom across different life experiences. Fathers can share their life lessons, challenges, and triumphs, offering their sons valuable insights that only come with time. By sharing their own vulnerabilities—such as fears, mistakes, and moments of uncertainty—

fathers can help normalize the human experience of struggle. This candid approach cultivates resilience in sons, teaching them that it is okay to face challenges and to seek help when needed.

In addition, as societal norms evolve, the role of effective communication becomes increasingly vital in addressing the specific challenges that Black men and boys may face today. Conversations about identity, race, mental health, and societal pressures can be tough, but they are necessary. Fathers who are willing to tackle these subjects openly empower their sons to confront the complexities of the world with confidence and clarity. Rather than allowing silence or avoidance to create barriers, proactive communication lays the groundwork for dialogue that can lead to understanding and empowerment.

The significance of communication in the father-son relationship is profound. By fostering open lines of dialogue and creating safe spaces for expression, fathers can build robust connections founded on trust, empathy, and understanding. The act of being an attentive listener and drawing out the deeper thoughts and feelings of their sons ultimately equips the next generation with the tools they need for emotional intelligence and resilience. As fathers commit to nurturing these conversations, they not only strengthen their relationship with their sons but also contribute positively to the development of confident, self-aware, and emotionally intelligent young men. This legacy of communication will echo through generations, creating a lasting impact on families and communities alike.

Ties to the Community and Spiritual Growth

Ties to the community and spiritual growth represent vital components in nurturing strong father-son relationships. As fathers actively engage with their communities alongside their sons, they not only foster a sense of belonging but also create memorable experiences that enhance their bond. Participating together in church activities, community service, and family support networks solidifies their relationship while imparting essential life lessons. This shared commitment gives both fathers and sons a common purpose, which can significantly bolster their emotional and spiritual connection.

In today's fast-paced world, it is all too easy for families to become isolated. Distractions abound—be it work commitments, social media, or the ever-pressing demands of daily life. However, by committing to involvement in community-focused activities, fathers and sons can step away from these distractions and ground themselves in shared experiences. Engaging together in meaningful service initiatives and church events provides a platform for dialogue and connection that may be more challenging to foster in the hustle and bustle of everyday life.

Hebrews 10:24-25 (NIV) serves as a powerful reminder of the importance of community and supports the significance of coming together for a higher purpose. It states, "And let us consider how we may spur one another on toward love and good deeds, not giving up meeting together, as some are in the habit of doing but encouraging one another." This scripture encourages fathers and sons to inspire each other, actively participating in their spiritual growth, and developing a greater understanding of their shared faith and values.

Joining in church activities can be particularly transformative in how fathers and sons perceive their roles within both their family and the broader community. These activities may include youth groups, prayer meetings, and service projects, where they work side by side, building a strong foundation for communication and understanding. They learn to appreciate each other's perspectives through shared experiences—whether preparing meals for the less fortunate, participating in outreach programs, or volunteering for local events. These moments of altruism promote not only spiritual growth but also reinforce the idea that their faith is best expressed through actions, love, and service.

Moreover, community service provides an opportunity for fathers to impart valuable life lessons to their sons. As fathers model selflessness and compassion through their interactions with others, sons learn the importance of giving back. They realize that making a positive impact on the world starts at home and extends to the community at large. This sense of responsibility fosters character development in sons and equips them with the foundational social skills necessary for future relationships.

Family support networks also play a crucial role in strengthening father-son relationships within the community. Connecting with other families allows fathers and sons to widen their circle of influence, share experiences, and form friendships. These support systems can offer guidance during difficult times and a sense of stability, where fathers and sons can learn from the successes and challenges faced by other families. Moreover, they reinforce the concept that no one is alone in their struggles and provide additional avenues for spiritual growth through shared experiences.

In a community-focused environment, fathers and sons can engage in meaningful conversations about their faith and beliefs. These discussions not only encourage critical thinking but also promote deeper understanding and reflection on their values. As they explore together the importance of love, kindness, and service, they cultivate a strong ethical foundation rooted in spiritual growth. When fathers invest the time to guide their sons through these conversations, they help shape their moral compass, ensuring that their values are aligned with the teachings of their faith and community.

Spiritual growth nurtured through community ties also teaches resilience. Times of hardship are inevitable, and when they arise, having a solid support system allows fathers and sons to navigate these challenges together. Through shared experiences within their community, they learn how to rely on each other for encouragement and strength, fostering a deep sense of trust. The lessons gleaned from overcoming obstacles together only serve to fortify their bond, creating a lasting impact on their relationship.

In addition, participating in community activities can deepen the spiritual connection between fathers and sons. Shared rituals, such as prayer, worship, and fellowship, cultivate a collective awareness of their faith. Fathers have the unique opportunity to help their sons understand spiritual teachings through relatable stories and real-life applications. As they navigate their spiritual journey arm-in-arm, they create a legacy of faith that spans generations.

Furthermore, shared activities within the community help fathers and sons develop essential social skills, such as effective communication, teamwork, and empathy. As they interact with a diverse range of people and confront various life situations, they learn to appreciate different perspectives and backgrounds. This understanding is significant in today's multicultural society, as it prepares sons to engage positively with the world around them and contribute to a more inclusive community.

Building strong ties to the community plays an integral role in enhancing father-son relationships and encouraging spiritual growth. Through participation in church activities, community service, and support networks, fathers and sons can experience shared purpose and connection. The encouragement found in scriptures like Hebrews 10:24-25 serves as a guiding light, urging them to spur one another on toward love and good deeds. The lessons learned through communal engagement not only foster emotional bonds but also equip both fathers and sons with the tools they need to thrive spiritually and socially in an ever-changing world. By nurturing these connections, they lay a foundation for a lifelong relationship steeped in love, understanding, and faith.

Role Reversal and Growth

As sons grow older, the dynamic of the father-son relationship can evolve into a more reciprocal mentorship. Sons can offer fresh perspectives and insights while fathers can learn from the experiences and viewpoints of their sons. This evolving relationship fosters mutual respect and deepens the emotional bond. Titus 2:6-8 (NIV) highlights the significance of modeling good deeds and integrity, underscoring that lessons can flow both ways.

Crisis Moments and Redemption

In moments of crisis—be it personal struggles, health issues, or external hardships—the bond between father and son can be profoundly tested. Yet, it is often in these moments that strength is built. Luke 1:37 (NIV) states, "For no word from God will ever fail." This scripture serves to remind us that during crises, faith can serve as a powerful anchor, leading father and son through their trials towards recovery and reconnection.

As we bring "Fathers and Sons Rising" to a close, it is essential to recognize that the journey of nurturing father-son relationships is ongoing. It is a journey marked by trials and triumphs, faith and learning. With Yahweh's guidance and the teachings of Jesus, Black fathers and sons can rise together, mending the fabric of their families and communities as they embody the principles of love, respect, and responsibility.

In embracing our roles as fathers and sons, we must commit to learning from the past while fearlessly stepping into the future. Every conversation, every moment of guidance, every shared fear and aspiration, contributes to a legacy that can uplift entire communities. Let us remember the powerful reminder from Psalm 127:3 (NIV): "Children are a heritage from the Lord, offspring a reward from him." Our roles as fathers and sons hold a divine purpose, one that reaches far beyond our immediate relationships and carries the potential to transform generations to come.

May this chapter inspire Black fathers and sons to rise together, hand in hand, fostering bonds grounded in faith, understanding, and enduring love. As we conclude this book, let it be a beginning—a beginning of renewed connections, deeper conversations, and unresolved healing. Let "Where's Your Father" not just be a question, but an invitation for all fathers and sons to rise, actively engage, and create a legacy that honors the past and dreams of a brighter future.

EPILOGUE
EMBRACING THE JOURNEY

As we close the chapters of "Where's Your Daddy," we step back and appreciate the journey we've undertaken together—a journey steeped in the rich tapestry of our experiences, heritage, and faith. Each chapter has illuminated the intricate relationship between fathers and sons, underscoring the struggles we navigate and the triumphs we celebrate. It's a dialogue not just about our individual stories but about the collective narrative of our community—one marked by resilience, strength, and an unwavering spirit rooted in our identity as Black men and boys, beloved creations of Yahweh.

In examining the experiences shared in these pages, we cannot overlook the profound impact of our spiritual lives in shaping who we are and who we aspire to be. Our faith is a guiding light amid the shadows of societal challenges, providing hope and encouragement where it may feel in short supply. We are reminded that even in the moments when earthly fathers may falter or be absent, we are never truly alone. As the Scriptures affirm, "When my father and my mother forsake me, then the Lord will take me up" (Psalm 27:10, KJV). In this promise lies our strength; it reinforces the extraordinary bond we share with our Heavenly Father.

The love of Yahweh, displayed through the grace of the Lord Jesus Christ, serves as a foundation upon which we build our relationships—both within our family units and across our communities. Christ exemplifies the ultimate fatherly love: sacrificial, nurturing, and steadfast. His presence encourages us to extend this same love to our sons, instilling in them the values of empathy, integrity, and purpose. As we strive to emulate His example, we not only strengthen our bonds with our children but also with our community and, ultimately, with God Himself.

As this book journey concludes, let us take time to reflect on the lessons learned and stories shared. Each chapter challenges us to embrace vulnerability, communicate authentically, and be present in the lives of our sons. The tears shed and the laughter shared echo the complexities of our relationships—yet they also illuminate the beautiful tapestry woven by the threads of trust, love, and faith.

We are called not only to be fathers but to be mentors, role models, and guides. Each of us has a role in nurturing the next generation—empowering them to rise above obstacles, challenge norms, and pursue their dreams with unwavering faith. Let's commit to actively seeking out one another, forging connections rooted in support and encouragement, just as Yahweh designs for us.

Let us carry the lessons of love, service, and community into the world. Let's take our rightful place as leaders, advocates, and fathers—first in our homes and then in our broader communities—reflecting the light of Christ in every interaction. Whether through direct service, our daily conversations, or our unique narratives, we can demonstrate the transformative power of love and faith.

As we step forward past these pages, may we find strength in our identity as Black men and boys, fortified by the love of Yahweh. May we remember that our stories are part of a larger story—a divine narrative inscribed by the Creator's hand—that speaks of redemption, hope, and legacy. Let this understanding guide us as we embrace our responsibilities with grace, knowing that we are never alone on this journey.

In the words of our ancestors who forged paths through trials, may we declare with resolve: "We are here, we are strong, and we are rooted in faith." Let this be more than a closing; let it be a rallying cry as we continue to walk in the light of our Lord, together. Where there has been a void, may we fill it with love, faith, and the unbreakable bond of fatherhood—one that not only resonates through our families but echoes throughout our communities for generations to come.

So, as we turn the last page of "Where's Your Daddy," let us remember that this is just the beginning. The work continues, and the mission of love and connection thrives. Go forth and spread this message of hope, faith, and community, embodying the essence of who we are as sons of the Most High.